The Poetry of by Alexander Pope

Volume VIII

Alexander Pope was born on May 21st, 1688 in London into a Catholic family.

His education was affected by the recent Test Acts, upholding the status of the Church of England and banning Catholics from teaching. In effect this meant his formal education was over by the age of 12 and Pope was to now immerse himself in classical literature and languages and to, in effect, educate himself.

From this age too he also suffered from numerous health problems including a type of tuberculosis (Pott's disease) which resulted in a stunted, deformed body. Only to grow to a height of 4' 6", with a severe hunchback and complicated further by respiratory difficulties, high fevers, inflamed eyes and abdominal pain all of which served to further isolate him, initially, from society.

However his talent was evident to all. Best known for his satirical verse, his translations of Homer and the use of the heroic couplet, he is the second-most frequently quoted writer in The Oxford Dictionary of Quotations, after Shakespeare.

With the publication of Pastorals in 1709 followed by An Essay on Criticism (1711) and his most famous work The Rape of the Lock (1712; revised and enlarged in 1714) Pope became not only famous but wealthy.

His translations of the Iliad and the Odyssey further enhanced both reputation and purse. His engagement to produce an opulent new edition of Shakespeare met with a mixed reception. Pope attempted to "regularise" Shakespeare's metre and rewrote some of his verse and cut 1500 lines, that Pope considered to be beneath the Bard's standard, to mere footnotes.

Alexander Pope died on May 30th, 1744 at his villa at Twickenham (where he created his famous grotto and gardens) and was buried in the nave of the nearby Church of England Church of St Mary the Virgin.

Over the years and centuries since his death Pope's work has been in and out of favour but with this distance he is now truly recognised as one of England's greatest poets.

Index of Contents

SAPPHO TO PHAON.

FROM THE FIFTEENTH OF OVID'S EPISTLES.

Say, lovely youth, that dost my heart command,
Can Phaon's eyes forget his Sappho's hand?
Must then her name the wretched writer prove,
To thy remembrance lost, as to thy love?
Ask not the cause that I new numbers choose,
The lute neglected and the lyric Muse;
Love taught my tears in sadder notes to flow,
And tuned my heart to elegies of woe,
I burn, I burn, as when through ripen'd corn
By driving winds the spreading flames are borne!
Phaon to Ætna's scorching fields retires,
While I consume with more than Ætna's fires!
No more my soul a charm in music finds;
Music has charms alone for peaceful minds.
Soft scenes of solitude no more can please;
Love enters there, and I'm my own disease.
No more the Lesbian dames my passion move,
Once the dear objects of my guilty love;
All other loves are lost in only thine,
Ah, youth ungrateful to a flame like mine!
Whom would not all those blooming charms surprise,
Those heavenly looks, and dear deluding eyes!
The harp and bow would you like Phoebus bear,
A brighter Phoebus Phaon might appear;
Would you with ivy wreath your flowing hair,
Not Bacchus' self with Phaon could compare:
Yet Phoebus loved, and Bacchus felt the flame,
One Daphne warm'd, and one the Cretan dame;
Nymphs that in verse no more could rival me,
Than e'en those gods contend in charms with thee.
The Muses teach me all their softest lays,
And the wide world resounds with Sappho's praise.
Though great Alcaeus more sublimely sings,
And strikes with bolder rage the sounding strings,
No less renown attends the moving lyre,
Which Venus tunes, and all her loves inspire.
To me what nature has in charms denied,
Is well by wit's more lasting flames supplied.
Though short my stature, yet my name extends

To heaven itself, and earth's remotest ends.
Brown as I am, an Ethiopian dame
Inspired young Perseus with a generous flame;
Turtles and doves of different hues unite,
And glossy jet is pair'd with shining white.
If to no charms thou wilt thy heart resign,
But such as merit, such as equal thine,
By none, alas! by none thou canst be moved,
Phaon alone by Phaon must be loved!
Yet once thy Sappho could thy cares employ,
Once in her arms you centred all your joy:
No time the dear remembrance can remove,
For, oh! how vast a memory has love!
My music, then, you could for ever hear,
And all my words were music to your ear.
You stopp'd with kisses my enchanting tongue,
And found my kisses sweeter than my song,
In all I pleased, but most in what was best;
And the last joy was dearer than the rest.
Then with each word, each glance, each motion fired,
You still enjoy'd, and yet you still desired,
Till, all dissolving, in the trance we lay,
And in tumultuous raptures died away.
The fair Sicilians now thy soul inflame;
Why was I born, ye gods, a Lesbian dame?
But ah, beware, Sicilian nymphs! nor boast
That wandering heart which I so lately lost;
Nor be with all those tempting words abused,
Those tempting words were all to Sappho used.
And you that rule Sicilia's happy plains,
Have pity, Venus, on your poet's pains!
Shall fortune still in one sad tenor run,
And still increase the woes so soon begun?
Inured to sorrow from my tender years,
My parents' ashes drank my early tears:
My brother next, neglecting wealth and fame,
Ignobly burn'd in a destructive flame:
An infant daughter late my griefs increased,
And all a mother's cares distract my breast,
Alas! what more could Fate itself impose,
But thee, the last, and greatest of my woes?
No more my robes in waving purple flow,
Nor on my hand the sparkling diamonds glow;
No more my locks in ringlets curl'd diffuse
The costly sweetness of Arabian dews,
Nor braids of gold the varied tresses bind,
That fly disorder'd with the wanton wind:
For whom should Sappho use such arts as these?

He's gone, whom only she desired to please!
Cupid's light darts my tender bosom move;
Still is there cause for Sappho still to love:
So from my birth the Sisters fix'd my doom,
And gave to Venus all my life to come;
Or, while my Muse in melting notes complains,
My yielding heart keeps measure to my strains.
By charms like thine, which all my soul have won,
Who might not—ah! who would not be undone?
For those Aurora Cephalus might scorn,
And with fresh blushes paint the conscious morn.
For those might Cynthia lengthen Phaon's sleep;
And bid Endymion nightly tend his sheep;
Venus for those had rapt thee to the skies;
But Mars on thee might look with Venus' eyes.
Oh scarce a youth, yet scarce a tender boy!
Oh useful time for lovers to employ!
Pride of thy age, and glory of thy race,
Come to these arms, and melt in this embrace!
The vows you never will return, receive;
And take, at least, the love you will not give.
See, while I write, my words are lost in tears!
The less my sense, the more my love appears.
Sure 'twas not much to bid one kind adieu,
(At least to feign was never hard to you)
'Farewell, my Lesbian love,' you might have said;
Or coldly thus, 'Farewell, O Lesbian maid!'
No tear did you, no parting kiss receive,
Nor knew I then how much I was to grieve.
No lover's gift your Sappho could confer,
And wrongs and woes were all you left with her.
No charge I gave you, and no charge could give,
But this, 'Be mindful of our loves, and live.'
Now by the Nine, those powers adored by me,
And Love, the god that ever waits on thee,
When first I heard (from whom I hardly knew)
That you were fled, and all my joys with you,
Like some sad statue, speechless, pale, I stood,
Grief chill'd my breast, and stopp'd my freezing blood;
No sigh to rise, no tear had power to flow,
Fix'd in a stupid lethargy of woe:
But when its way the impetuous passion found,
I rend my tresses, and my breast I wound:
I rave, then weep; I curse, and then complain;
Now swell to rage, now melt in tears again.
Not fiercer pangs distract the mournful dame,
Whose first-born infant feeds the funeral flame.
My scornful brother with a smile appears,

Insults my woes, and triumphs in my tears;
His hated image ever haunts my eyes;
'And why this grief? thy daughter lives!' he cries.
Stung with my love, and furious with despair,
All torn my garments, and my bosom bare,
My woes, thy crimes, I to the world proclaim;
Such inconsistent things are love and shame!
'Tis thou art all my care and my delight,
My daily longing, and my dream by night;
Oh night more pleasing than the brightest day,
When fancy gives what absence takes away,
And, dress'd in all its visionary charms,
Restores my fair deserter to my arms!
Then round your neck in wanton wreaths I twine,
Then you, methinks, as fondly circle mine:
A thousand tender words I hear and speak;
A thousand melting kisses give and take:
Then fiercer joys, I blush to mention these,
Yet, while I blush, confess how much they please.
But when, with day, the sweet delusions fly,
And all things wake to life and joy but I,
As if once more forsaken, I complain,
And close my eyes to dream of you again:
Then frantic rise, and like some Fury rove
Through lonely plains, and through the silent grove;
As if the silent grove, and lonely plains,
That knew my pleasures, could relieve my pains.
I view the grotto, once the scene of love,
The rocks around, the hanging roofs above,
That charm'd me more, with native moss o'ergrown,
Than Phrygian marble, or the Parian stone;
I find the shades that veil'd our joys before;
But, Phaon gone, those shades delight no more.
Here the press'd herbs with bending tops betray
Where oft entwined in amorous folds we lay;
I kiss that earth which once was press'd by you,
And all with tears the withering herbs bedew.
For thee the fading trees appear to mourn,
And birds defer their songs till thy return:
Night shades the groves, and all in silence lie,
All but the mournful Philomel and I:
With mournful Philomel I join my strain,
Of Tereus she, of Phaon I complain.

A spring there is, whose silver waters show,
Clear as a glass, the shining sands below:
A flowery lotus spreads its arms above,
Shades all the banks, and seems itself a grove;

Eternal greens the mossy margin grace,
Watch'd by the sylvan genius of the place.
Here as I lay, and swell'd with tears the flood,
Before my sight a watery virgin stood:
She stood and cried, 'O you that love in vain!
Fly hence, and seek the fair Leucadian main;
There stands a rock, from whose impending steep
Apollo's fane surveys the rolling deep;
There injured lovers, leaping from above,
Their flames extinguish, and forget to love.
Deucalion once with hopeless fury burn'd,
In vain he loved, relentless Pyrrha scorn'd:
But when from hence he plunged into the main,
Deucalion scorn'd, and Pyrrha loved in vain.
Haste, Sappho, haste, from high Leucadia throw
Thy wretched weight, nor dread the deeps below!'
She spoke, and vanish'd with the voice—I rise,
And silent tears fall trickling from my eyes.
I go, ye nymphs! those rocks and seas to prove;
How much I fear, but ah, how much I love!
I go, ye nymphs! where furious love inspires:
Let female fears submit to female fires.
To rocks and seas I fly from Phaon's hate,
And hope from seas and rocks a milder fate.
Ye gentle gales, beneath my body blow,
And softly lay me on the waves below!
And thou, kind Love, my sinking limbs sustain,
Spread thy soft wings, and waft me o'er the main,
Nor let a lover's death the guiltless flood profane!
On Phoebus' shrine my harp I'll then bestow,
And this inscription shall be placed below:
'Here she who sung, to him that did inspire,
Sappho to Phoebus consecrates her lyre;
What suits with Sappho, Phoebus, suits with thee:
The gift, the giver, and the god agree.'

But why, alas! relentless youth, ah, why
To distant seas must tender Sappho fly?
Thy charms than those may far more powerful be,
And Phoebus' self is less a god to me.
Ah! canst thou doom me to the rocks and sea,
Oh far more faithless and more hard than they?
Ah! canst thou rather see this tender breast
Dash'd on these rocks than to thy bosom press'd?
This breast which once, in vain, you liked so well;
Where the Loves play'd, and where the Muses dwell.
Alas! the Muses now no more inspire;
Untuned my lute, and silent is my lyre.

My languid numbers have forgot to flow,
And fancy sinks beneath a weight of woe.
Ye Lesbian virgins, and ye Lesbian dames,
Themes of my verse, and objects of my flames,
No more your groves with my glad songs shall ring,
No more these hands shall touch the trembling string:
My Phaon's fled, and I those arts resign;
(Wretch that I am, to call that Phaon mine!)
Return, fair youth! return, and bring along
Joy to my soul, and vigour to my song:
Absent from thee, the poet's flame expires;
But ah! how fiercely burn the lover's fires?
Gods! can no prayers, no sighs, no numbers move
One savage heart, or teach it how to love?
The winds my prayers, my sighs, my numbers bear,
The flying winds have lost them all in air!
Oh when, alas! shall more auspicious gales
To these fond eyes restore thy welcome sails?
If you return—ah, why these long delays?
Poor Sappho dies while careless Phaon stays.
Oh launch thy bark, nor fear the watery plain;
Venus for thee shall smooth her native main.
Oh launch thy bark, secure of prosperous gales;
Cupid for thee shall spread the swelling sails.
If you will fly—(yet ah! what cause can be,
Too cruel youth, that you should fly from me?)
If not from Phaon I must hope for ease,
Ah, let me seek it from the raging seas:
To raging seas unpitied I'll remove,
And either cease to live, or cease to love!

THE FABLE OF DRYOPE.

FROM THE NINTH BOOK OF OVID'S METAMORPHOSES.

She said, and for her lost Galanthis sighs;
When the fair consort of her son replies:
'Since you a servant's ravish'd form bemoan,
And kindly sigh for sorrows not your own,
Let me (if tears and grief permit) relate
A nearer woe, a sister's stranger fate.
No nymph of all Oechalia could compare
For beauteous form with Dryope the fair,
Her tender mother's only hope and pride,
(Myself the offspring of a second bride).
This nymph, compress'd by him who rules the day,

Whom Delphi and the Delian isle obey,
Andraemon loved; and, bless'd in all those charms
That pleased a god, succeeded to her arms.

'A lake there was with shelving banks around,
Whose verdant summit fragrant myrtles crown'd.
These shades, unknowing of the fates, she sought,
And to the Naiads flowery garlands brought:
Her smiling babe (a pleasing charge) she press'd
Within her arms, and nourish'd at her breast.
Not distant far, a watery lotus grows;
The spring was new, and all the verdant boughs,
Adorn'd with blossoms, promised fruits that vie
In glowing colours with the Tyrian dye:
Of these she cropp'd, to please her infant son,
And I myself the same rash act had done:
But, lo! I saw (as near her side I stood)
The violated blossoms drop with blood;
Upon the tree I cast a frightful look;
The trembling tree with sudden horror shook.
Lotis the nymph (if rural tales be true)
As from Priapus' lawless lust she flew,
Forsook her form, and, fixing here, became
A flowery plant, which still preserves her name.

'This change unknown, astonish'd at the sight,
My trembling sister strove to urge her flight;
And first the pardon of the nymphs implored,
And those offended sylvan powers adored:
But when she backward would have fled, she found
Her stiffening feet were rooted in the ground:
In vain to free her fasten'd feet she strove,
And as she struggles only moves above;
She feels th' encroaching bark around her grow
By quick degrees, and cover all below:
Surprised at this, her trembling hand she heaves
To rend her hair; her hand is fill'd with leaves:
Where late was hair, the shooting leaves are seen
To rise, and shade her with a sudden green.
The child Amphissus, to her bosom press'd,
Perceived a colder and a harder breast,
And found the springs, that ne'er till then denied
Their milky moisture, on a sudden dried.
I saw, unhappy! what I now relate,
And stood the helpless witness of thy fate;
Embraced thy boughs, thy rising bark delay'd,
There wish'd to grow, and mingle shade with shade.

'Behold Andraemon and th' unhappy sire
Appear, and for their Dryope inquire:
A springing tree for Dryope they find,
And print warm kisses on the panting rind,
Prostrate, with tears their kindred plant bedew,
And close embrace as to the roots they grew.
The face was all that now remain'd of thee,
No more a woman, nor yet quite a tree;
Thy branches hung with humid pearls appear,
From every leaf distils a trickling tear;
And straight a voice, while yet a voice remains,
Thus through the trembling boughs in sighs complains:

'"If to the wretched any faith be given,
I swear by all th' unpitying powers of Heaven,
No wilful crime this heavy vengeance bred;
In mutual innocence our lives we led:
If this be false, let these new greens decay,
Let sounding axes lop my limbs away,
And crackling flames on all my honours prey.
But from my branching arms this infant bear,
Let some kind nurse supply a mother's care:
And to his mother let him oft be led,
Sport in her shades, and in her shades be fed:
Teach him, when first his infant voice shall frame
Imperfect words, and lisp his mother's name,
To hail this tree, and say, with weeping eyes,
'Within this plant my hapless parent lies:'
And when in youth he seeks the shady woods,
Oh! let him fly the crystal lakes and floods,
Nor touch the fatal flowers; but, warn'd by me,
Believe a goddess shrined in every tree.
My sire, my sister, and my spouse, farewell!
If in your breasts or love or pity dwell,
Protect your plant, nor let my branches feel
The browsing cattle or the piercing steel.
Farewell! and since I cannot bend to join
My lips to yours, advance at least to mine.
My son, thy mother's parting kiss receive,
While yet thy mother has a kiss to give.
I can no more; the creeping rind invades
My closing lips, and hides my head in shades:
Remove your hands, the bark shall soon suffice
Without their aid to seal these dying eyes."

'She ceased at once to speak and ceased to be,
And all the nymph was lost within the tree;
Yet latent life through her new branches reign'd,

And long the plant a human heat retain'd.'

VERTUMNUS AND POMONA,

FROM THE FOURTEENTH BOOK OF OVID'S METAMORPHOSES.

The fair Pomona flourish'd in his reign;
Of all the virgins of the sylvan train
None taught the trees a nobler race to bear,
Or more improved the vegetable care.
To her the shady grove, the flowery field,
The streams and fountains no delights could yield:
'Twas all her joy the ripening fruits to tend,
And see the boughs with happy burdens bend.
The hook she bore instead of Cynthia's spear,
To lop the growth of the luxuriant year,
To decent forms the lawless shoots to bring,
And teach th' obedient branches where to spring.
Now the cleft rind inserted grafts receives,
And yields an offspring more than nature gives;
Now sliding streams the thirsty plants renew,
And feed their fibres with reviving dew.

These cares alone her virgin breast employ,
Averse from Venus and the nuptial joy.
Her private orchards, wall'd on every side,
To lawless sylvans all access denied.
How oft the satyrs and the wanton fauns,
Who haunt the forests or frequent the lawns,
The god whose ensign scares the birds of prey,
And old Silenus, youthful in decay,
Employ'd their wiles and unavailing care
To pass the fences, and surprise the fair!
Like these, Vertumnus own'd his faithful flame,
Like these, rejected by the scornful dame.
To gain her sight a thousand forms he wears;
And first a reaper from the field appears:
Sweating he walks, while loads of golden grain
O'ercharge the shoulders of the seeming swain:
Oft o'er his back a crooked scythe is laid,
And wreaths of hay his sunburnt temples shade:
Oft in his harden'd hand a goad he bears,
Like one who late unyoked the sweating steers:
Sometimes his pruning-hook corrects the vines,
And the loose stragglers to their ranks confines:
Now gathering what the bounteous year allows,

He pulls ripe apples from the bending boughs:
A soldier now, he with his sword appears;
A fisher next, his trembling angle bears:
Each shape he varies, and each art he tries,
On her bright charms to feast his longing eyes.

A female form at last Vertumnus wears,
With all the marks of reverend age appears,
His temples thinly spread with silver hairs:
Propp'd on his staff, and stooping as he goes,
A painted mitre shades his furrow'd brows.
The god in this decrepid form array'd
The gardens enter'd, and the fruit survey'd;
And, 'Happy you!' he thus address'd the maid,
'Whose charms as far all other nymphs outshine,
As other gardens are excell'd by thine!'
Then kiss'd the fair; (his kisses warmer grow
Than such as women on their sex bestow)
Then, placed beside her on the flowery ground,
Beheld the trees with autumn's bounty crown'd.
An elm was near, to whose embraces led,
The curling vine her swelling clusters spread:
He view'd her twining branches with delight,
And praised the beauty of the pleasing sight.

'Yet this tall elm, but for this vine,' he said,
'Had stood neglected, and a barren shade;
And this fair vine, but that her arms surround
Her married elm, had crept along the ground.
Ah, beauteous maid! let this example move
Your mind, averse from all the joys of love.
Deign to be loved, and every heart subdue!
What nymph could e'er attract such crowds as you?
Not she whose beauty urged the Centaur's arms,
Ulysses' queen, nor Helen's fatal charms.
Ev'n now, when silent scorn is all they gain,
A thousand court you, though they court in vain—
A thousand sylvans, demigods, and gods,
That haunt our mountains and our Alban woods.
But if you'll prosper, mark what I advise,
Whom age and long experience render wise,
And one whose tender care is far above
All that these lovers ever felt of love,
(Far more than e'er can by yourself be guess'd)
Fix on Vertumnus, and reject the rest:
For his firm faith I dare engage my own:
Scarce to himself, himself is better known.
To distant lands Vertumnus never roves;

Like you, contented with his native groves;
Nor at first sight, like most, admires the fair:
For you he lives; and you alone shall share
His last affection, as his early care.
Besides, he's lovely far above the rest,
With youth immortal, and with beauty bless'd.
Add, that he varies every shape with ease,
And tries all forms that may Pomona please.
But what should most excite a mutual flame,
Your rural cares and pleasures are the same.
To him your orchard's early fruits are due;
(A pleasing offering when 'tis made by you)
He values these; but yet, alas! complains
That still the best and dearest gift remains.
Not the fair fruit that on yon branches glows
With that ripe red th' autumnal sun bestows;
Nor tasteful herbs that in these gardens rise,
Which the kind soil with milky sap supplies;
You, only you, can move the god's desire:
Oh crown so constant and so pure a fire!
Let soft compassion touch your gentle mind:
Think, 'tis Vertumnus begs you to be kind:
So may no frost, when early buds appear,
Destroy the promise of the youthful year;
Nor winds, when first your florid orchard blows,
Shake the light blossoms from their blasted boughs!'

This, when the various god had urged in vain,
He straight assumed his native form again:
Such, and so bright an aspect now he bears,
As when through clouds th' emerging sun appears,
And thence exerting his refulgent ray,
Dispels the darkness, and reveals the day.
Force he prepared, but check'd the rash design;
For when, appearing in a form divine,
The nymph surveys him, and beholds the grace
Of charming features and a youthful face,
In her soft breast consenting passions move,
And the warm maid confess'd a mutual love.

THE FIRST BOOK OF STATIUS'S THEBAIS.

TRANSLATED IN THE YEAR 1703.

ARGUMENT.

Oedipus, King of Thebes, having, by mistake, slain his father Laius, and married his mother Jocasta, put out his own eyes, and resigned his realm to his sons Eteocles and Polynices. Being neglected by them, he makes his prayer to the fury Tisiphone, to sow debate betwixt the brothers. They agree at last to reign singly, each a year by turns, and the first lot is obtained by Eteocles. Jupiter, in a council of the gods, declares his resolution of punishing the Thebans, and Argives also, by means of a marriage betwixt Polynices and one of the daughters of Adrastus, King of Argos. Juno opposes, but to no effect; and Mercury is sent on a message to the shades, to the ghost of Laius, who is to appear to Eteocles, and provoke him to break the agreement. Polynices, in the meantime, departs from Thebes by night, is overtaken by a storm, and arrives at Argos, where he meets with Tydeus, who had fled from Calydon, having killed his brother. Adrastus entertains them, having received an oracle from Apollo that his daughters should be married to a boar and a lion, which he understands to be meant by these strangers, by whom the hides of those beasts were worn, and who arrived at the time when he kept an annual feast in honour of that god. The rise of this solemnity, he relates to his guests; the loves of Phoebus and Psamathe, and the story of Choroebus. He inquires, and is made acquainted with their descent and quality. The sacrifice is renewed, and the book concludes with a hymn to Apollo.

Fraternal rage, the guilty Thebes' alarms,
Th' alternate reign destroy'd by impious arms,
Demand our song; a sacred fury fires
My ravish'd breast, and all the Muse inspires.
O goddess! say, shall I deduce my rhymes
From the dire nation in its early times,
Europa's rape, Agenor's stern decree,
And Cadmus searching round the spacious sea?
How with the serpent's teeth he sow'd the soil,
And reap'd an iron harvest of his toil?
Or how from joining stones the city sprung,
While to his harp divine Amphion sung?
Or shall I Juno's hate to Thebes resound,
Whose fatal rage th' unhappy monarch found?
The sire against the son his arrows drew,
O'er the wide fields the furious mother flew,
And while her arms a second hope contain,
Sprung from the rocks, and plunged into the main.

But wave whate'er to Cadmus may belong,
And fix, O Muse! the barrier of thy song
At Oedipus—from his disasters trace
The long confusions of his guilty race:
Nor yet attempt to stretch thy bolder wing,
And mighty Caesar's conquering eagles sing;
How twice he tamed proud Ister's rapid flood,
While Dacian mountains stream'd with barbarous blood;
Twice taught the Rhine beneath his laws to roll,
And stretch'd his empire to the frozen pole;
Or, long before, with early valour strove
In youthful arms t' assert the cause of Jove.
And thou, great heir of all thy father's fame,

Increase of glory to the Latian name!
Oh! bless thy Rome with an eternal reign,
Nor let desiring worlds entreat in vain.
What though the stars contract their heavenly space,
And crowd their shining ranks to yield thee place;
Though all the skies, ambitious of thy sway,
Conspire to court thee from our world away;
Though Phoebus longs to mix his rays with thine,
And in thy glories more serenely shine;
Though Jove himself no less content would be
To part his throne, and share his heaven with thee:
Yet stay, great Cæsar! and vouchsafe to reign
O'er the wide earth, and o'er the watery main;
Resign to Jove his empire of the skies,
And people heaven with Roman deities.

The time will come when a diviner flame
Shall warm my breast to sing of Cæsar's fame;
Meanwhile, permit that my preluding Muse
In Theban wars an humbler theme may choose:
Of furious hate surviving death she sings,
A fatal throne to two contending kings,
And funeral flames, that, parting wide in air,
Express the discord of the souls they bear:
Of towns dispeopled, and the wandering ghosts
Of kings unburied in the wasted coasts;
When Dirce's fountain blush'd with Grecian blood,
And Thetis, near Ismenos' swelling flood,
With dread beheld the rolling surges sweep
In heaps his slaughter'd sons into the deep.

What hero, Clio! wilt thou first relate?
The rage of Tydeus, or the prophet's fate?
Or how, with hills of slain on every side,
Hippomedon repell'd the hostile tide?
Or how the youth, with every grace adorn'd,
Untimely fell, to be for ever mourn'd?
Then to fierce Capaneus thy verse extend,
And sing with horror his prodigious end.

Now wretched Oedipus, deprived of sight,
Led a long death in everlasting night;
But while he dwells where not a cheerful ray
Can pierce the darkness, and abhors the day,
The clear reflecting mind presents his sin
In frightful views, and makes it day within;
Returning thoughts in endless circles roll,
And thousand Furies haunt his guilty soul:

The wretch then lifted to th' unpitying skies
Those empty orbs from whence he tore his eyes,
Whose wounds, yet fresh, with bloody hands he strook,
While from his breast these dreadful accents broke:

'Ye gods! that o'er the gloomy regions reign,
Where guilty spirits feel eternal pain;
Thou, sable Styx! whose livid streams are roll'd
Through dreary coasts, which I though blind behold;
Tisiphone! that oft hast heard my prayer,
Assist, if Oedipus deserve thy care.
If you received me from Jocasta's womb,
And nursed the hope of mischiefs yet to come;
If, leaving Polybus, I took my way
To Cyrrha's temple, on that fatal day
When by the son the trembling father died,
Where the three roads the Phocian fields divide;
If I the Sphynx's riddles durst explain,
Taught by thyself to win the promised reign;
If wretched I, by baleful Furies led,
With monstrous mixture stain'd my mother's bed,
For hell and thee begot an impious brood,
And with full lust those horrid joys renew'd;
Then, self-condemn'd to shades of endless night,
Forced from these orbs the bleeding balls of sight;
Oh, hear! and aid the vengeance I require,
If worthy thee, and what thou might'st inspire!
My sons their old, unhappy sire despise,
Spoil'd of his kingdom, and deprived of eyes;
Guideless I wander, unregarded mourn,
Whilst these exalt their sceptres o'er my urn:
These sons, ye gods! who with flagitious pride
Insult my darkness and my groans deride.
Art thou a father, unregarding Jove!
And sleeps thy thunder in the realms above?
Thou Fury! then some lasting curse entail,
Which o'er their children's children shall prevail;
Place on their heads that crown, distain'd with gore,
Which these dire hands from my slain father tore;
Go! and a parent's heavy curses bear;
Break all the bonds of nature, and prepare
Their kindred souls to mutual hate and war.
Give them to dare, what I might wish to see,
Blind as I am, some glorious villany!
Soon shalt thou find, if thou but arm their hands,
Their ready guilt preventing thy commands:
Couldst thou some great proportion'd mischief frame,
They'd prove the father from whose loins they came.'

The Fury heard, while on Cocytus' brink
Her snakes, untied, sulphureous waters drink;
But at the summons roll'd her eyes around,
And snatch'd the starting serpents from the ground.
Not half so swiftly shoots along in air
The gliding lightning or descending star;
Through crowds of airy shades she wing'd her flight,
And dark dominions of the silent night;
Swift as she pass'd the flitting ghosts withdrew,
And the pale spectres trembled at her view:
To th' iron gates of Tenarus she flies,
There spreads her dusky pinions to the skies.
The day beheld, and, sickening at the sight,
Veil'd her fair glories in the shades of night.
Affrighted Atlas on the distant shore
Trembled, and shook the heavens and gods he bore.
Now from beneath Malea's airy height
Aloft she sprung, and steer'd to Thebes her flight;
With eager speed the well-known journey took,
Nor here regrets the hell she late forsook.
A hundred snakes her gloomy visage shade,
A hundred serpents guard her horrid head;
In her sunk eyeballs dreadful meteors glow:
Such rays from Phoebe's bloody circle flow,
When, labouring with strong charms, she shoots from high
A fiery gleam, and reddens all the sky.
Blood stain'd her cheeks, and from her mouth there came
Blue steaming poisons, and a length of flame.
From every blast of her contagious breath
Famine and drought proceed, and plagues and death.
A robe obscene was o'er her shoulders thrown,
A dress by Fates and Furies worn alone.
She toss'd her meagre arms; her better hand
In waving circles whirl'd a funeral brand:
A serpent from her left was seen to rear
His flaming crest, and lash the yielding air.
But when the Fury took her stand on high,
Where vast Cithæron's top salutes the sky,
A hiss from all the snaky tire went round:
The dreadful signal all the rocks rebound,
And through th' Achaian cities send the sound.
Oete, with high Parnassus, heard the voice;
Eurotas' banks remurmur'd to the noise;
Again Leucothoë shook at these alarms,
And press'd Palærmon closer in her arms.
Headlong from thence the glowing Fury springs,
And o'er the Theban palace spreads her wings,

Once more invades the guilty dome, and shrouds
Its bright pavilions in a veil of clouds.
Straight with the rage of all their race possess'd,
Stung to the soul, the brothers start from rest,
And all their Furies wake within their breast:
Their tortured minds repining Envy tears,
And Hate, engender'd by suspicious fears:
And sacred thirst of sway, and all the ties
Of nature broke; and royal perjuries;
And impotent desire to reign alone,
That scorns the dull reversion of a throne:
Each would the sweets of sovereign rule devour,
While Discord waits upon divided power.

As stubborn steers, by brawny ploughmen broke,
And join'd reluctant to the galling yoke,
Alike disdain with servile necks to bear
Th' unwonted weight, or drag the crooked share,
But rend the reins, and bound a different way,
And all the furrows in confusion lay:
Such was the discord of the royal pair
Whom fury drove precipitate to war.
In vain the chiefs contrived a specious way
To govern Thebes by their alternate sway:
Unjust decree! while this enjoys the state,
That mourns in exile his unequal fate,
And the short monarch of a hasty year
Foresees with anguish his returning heir.
Thus did the league their impious arms restrain,
But scarce subsisted to the second reign.

Yet then no proud aspiring piles were raised,
No fretted roofs with polish'd metals blazed;
No labour'd columns in long order placed,
No Grecian stone the pompous arches graced:
No nightly bands in glittering armour wait
Before the sleepless tyrant's guarded gate;
No chargers then were wrought in burnish'd gold,
Nor silver vases took the forming mould;
Nor gems on bowls emboss'd were seen to shine,
Blaze on the brims, and sparkle in the wine—
Say, wretched rivals! what provokes your rage?
Say, to what end your impious arms engage?
Not all bright Phoebus views in early morn,
Or when his evening beams the west adorn,
When the south glows with his meridian ray,
And the cold north receives a fainter day;
For crimes like these, not all those realms suffice,

Were all those realms the guilty victor's prize!

But Fortune now (the lots of empire thrown)
Decrees to proud Eteocles the crown:
What joys, O tyrant! swell'd thy soul that day,
When all were slaves thou couldst around survey,
Pleased to behold unbounded power thy own,
And singly fill a fear'd and envied throne!

But the vile vulgar, ever discontent,
Their growing fears in secret murmurs vent;
Still prone to change, though still the slaves of state,
And sure the monarch whom they have, to hate;
New lords they madly make, then tamely bear,
And softly curse the tyrants whom they fear.
And one of those who groan beneath the sway
Of kings imposed, and grudgingly obey,
(Whom envy to the great, and vulgar spite,
With scandal arm'd, th' ignoble mind's delight)
Exclaim'd—'O Thebes! for thee what fates remain,
What woes attend this inauspicious reign?
Must we, alas! our doubtful necks prepare
Each haughty master's yoke by turns to bear,
And still to change whom changed we still must fear?
These now control a wretched people's fate
These can divide, and these reverse the state:
E'en fortune rules no more—O servile land,
Where exiled tyrants still by turns command!
Thou sire of gods and men, imperial Jove!
Is this th' eternal doom decreed above?
On thy own offspring hast thou fix'd this fate
From the first birth of our unhappy state,
When banish'd Cadmus, wandering o'er the main,
For lost Europa search'd the world in vain,
And, fated in Boeotian fields to found,
A rising empire on a foreign ground,
First raised our walls on that ill omen'd plain
Where earth-born brothers were by brothers slain?
What lofty looks th' unrivall'd monarch bears!
How all the tyrant in his face appears!
What sullen fury clouds his scornful brow!
Gods! how his eyes with threatening ardour glow!
Can this imperious lord forget to reign,
Quit all his state, descend, and serve again?
Yet who, before, more popularly bow'd?
Who more propitious to the suppliant crowd?
Patient of right, familiar in the throne,
What wonder then? he was not then alone.

Oh wretched we! a vile, submissive train,
Fortune's tame fools, and slaves in every reign!

'As when two winds with rival force contend,
This way and that the wavering sails they bend,
While freezing Boreas and black Eurus blow,
Now here, now there, the reeling vessel throw;
Thus on each side, alas! our tottering state
Feels all the fury of resistless fate,   0
And doubtful still, and still distracted stands,
While that prince threatens, and while this commands.'

And now th' almighty Father of the gods
Convenes a council in the bless'd abodes.
Far in the bright recesses of the skies,
High o'er the rolling heavens, a mansion lies,
Whence, far below, the gods at once survey
The realms of rising and declining day,
And all th' extended space of earth, and air, and sea.
Full in the midst, and on a starry throne,
The Majesty of heaven superior shone:
Serene he look'd, and gave an awful nod,
And all the trembling spheres confess'd the god.
At Jove's assent the deities around
In solemn state the consistory crown'd.
Next a long order of inferior powers
Ascend from hills, and plains, and shady bowers;
Those from whose urns the rolling rivers flow,
And those that give the wandering winds to blow:
Here all their rage and ev'n their murmurs cease,
And sacred silence reigns, and universal peace.
A shining synod of majestic gods
Gilds with new lustre the divine abodes:
Heaven seems improved with a superior ray,
And the bright arch reflects a double day.
The monarch then his solemn silence broke,
The still creation listen'd while he spoke;
Each sacred accent bears eternal weight,
And each irrevocable word is fate.

'How long shall man the wrath of Heaven defy,
And force unwilling vengeance from the sky?
O race confederate into crimes, that prove
Triumphant o'er th' eluded rage of Jove!
This wearied arm can scarce the bolt sustain,
And unregarded thunder rolls in vain:
Th' o'erlabour'd Cyclops from his task retires,
Th' AEolian forge exhausted of its fires.

For this, I suffer'd Phoebus' steeds to stray,
And the mad ruler to misguide the day,
When the wide earth to heaps of ashes turn'd,
And Heaven itself the wandering chariot burn'd:
For this my brother of the watery reign
Released the impetuous sluices of the main;
But flames consumed, and billows raged in vain.
Two races now, allied to Jove, offend;
To punish these, see Jove himself descend.
The Theban kings their line from Cadmus trace,
From godlike Perseus those of Argive race.
Unhappy Cadmus' fate who does not know,
And the long series of succeeding woe?
How oft the Furies, from the deeps of night,
Arose, and mix'd with men in mortal fight;
Th' exulting mother stain'd with filial blood,
The savage hunter and the haunted wood?
The direful banquet why should I proclaim,
And crimes that grieve the trembling gods to name?
Ere I recount the sins of these profane,
The sun would sink into the western main,
And, rising, gild the radiant east again.
Have we not seen (the blood of Laius shed)
The murdering son ascend his parent's bed,
Through violated nature force his way,
And stain the sacred womb where once he lay?
Yet now in darkness and despair he groans,
And for the crimes of guilty fate atones;
His sons with scorn their eyeless father view,
Insult his wounds, and make them bleed anew.
Thy curse, O OEdipus! just Heaven alarms,
And sets th' avenging Thunderer in arms.
I from the root thy guilty race will tear,
And give the nations to the waste of war.
Adrastus soon, with gods averse, shall join
In dire alliance with the Theban line;
Hence strife shall rise, and mortal war succeed;
The guilty realms of Tantalus shall bleed:
Fix'd is their doom. This all-remembering breast
Yet harbours vengeance for the tyrant's feast.'

He said; and thus the queen of heaven return'd:
(With sudden grief her labouring bosom burn'd)
'Must I, whose cares Phoroneus' towers defend,
Must I, O Jove! in bloody wars contend?
Thou know'st those regions my protection claim,
Glorious in arms, in riches, and in fame:
Though there the fair Egyptian heifer fed,

And there deluded Argus slept and bled:
Though there the brazen tower was storm'd of old,
When Jove descended in almighty gold!
Yet I can pardon those obscurer rapes,
Those bashful crimes disguised in borrow'd shapes;
But Thebes, where, shining in celestial charms,
Thou cam'st triumphant to a mortal's arms,
When all my glories o'er her limbs were spread,
And blazing lightnings danced around her bed;
Cursed Thebes the vengeance it deserves may prove—
Ah! why should Argos feel the rage of Jove?
Yet since thou wilt thy sister-queen control,
Since still the lust of discord fires thy soul,
Go, raze my Samos, let Mycene fall,
And level with the dust the Spartan wall;
No more let mortals Juno's power invoke,
Her fanes no more with Eastern incense smoke,
Nor victims sink beneath the sacred stroke!
But to your Isis all my rights transfer,
Let altars blaze and temples smoke for her;
For her, through Egypt's fruitful clime renown'd,
Let weeping Nilus hear the timbrel sound.
But if thou must reform the stubborn times,
Avenging on the sons the fathers' crimes,
And from the long records of distant age
Derive incitements to renew thy rage;
Say, from what period then has Jove design'd
To date his vengeance? to what bounds confined?
Begin from thence, where first Alpheus hides
His wandering stream, and through the briny tides
Unmix'd to his Sicilian river glides.
Thy own Arcadians there the thunder claim,
Whose impious rites disgrace thy mighty name;
Who raise thy temples where the chariot stood
Of fierce Oenomaüs, defiled with blood;
Where once his steeds their savage banquet found,
And human bones yet whiten all the ground.
Say, can those honours please? and canst thou love
Presumptuous Crete, that boasts the tomb of Jove?
And shall not Tantalus's kingdoms share
Thy wife and sister's tutelary care?
Reverse, O Jove! thy too severe decree,
Nor doom to war a race derived from thee;
On impious realms and barbarous kings impose
Thy plagues, and curse them with such sons as those.'

Thus in reproach and prayer the queen express'd
The rage and grief contending in her breast;

Unmoved remain'd the ruler of the sky,
And from his throne return'd this stern reply:
"Twas thus I deem'd thy haughty soul would bear
The dire, though just revenge which I prepare
Against a nation thy peculiar care:
No less Dione might for Thebes contend.
Nor Bacchus less his native town defend;
Yet these in silence see the Fates fulfil
Their work, and reverence our superior will:
For by the black infernal Styx I swear,
(That dreadful oath which binds the Thunderer)
'Tis fix'd, th' irrevocable doom of Jove;
No force can bend me, no persuasion more.
Haste then, Cyllenius, through the liquid air;
Go, mount the winds, and to the shades repair;
Bid hell's black monarch my commands obey,
And give up Laius to the realms of day,
Whose ghost yet shivering on Cocytus' sand
Expects its passage to the further strand:
Let the pale sire revisit Thebes, and bear
These pleasing orders to the tyrant's ear;
That, from his exiled brother, swell'd with pride
Of foreign forces and his Argive bride,
Almighty Jove commands him to detain
The promised empire, and alternate reign:
Be this the cause of more than mortal hate;
The rest, succeeding times shall ripen into fate.'

The god obeys, and to his feet applies
Those golden wings that cut the yielding skies;
His ample hat his beamy locks o'erspread,
And veil'd the starry glories of his head.
He seized the wand that causes sleep to fly,
Or in soft slumbers seals the wakeful eye;
That drives the dead to dark Tartarean coasts,
Or back to life compels the wandering ghosts.
Thus through the parting clouds the son of May
Wings on the whistling winds his rapid way;
Now smoothly steers through air his equal flight,
Now springs aloft, and towers th' ethereal height:
Then wheeling down the steep of heaven he flies,
And draws a radiant circle o'er the skies.

Meantime the banish'd Polynices roves
(His Thebes abandon'd) through the Aonian groves,
While future realms his wandering thoughts delight,
His daily vision, and his dream by night;
Forbidden Thebes appears before his eye,

From whence he sees his absent brother fly,
With transport views the airy rule his own,
And swells on an imaginary throne.
Fain would he cast a tedious age away,
And live out all in one triumphant day.
He chides the lazy progress of the sun,
And bids the year with swifter motion run:
With anxious hopes his craving mind is toss'd
And all his joys in length of wishes lost.

The hero then resolves his course to bend
Where ancient Danaus' fruitful fields extend;
And famed Mycene's lofty towers ascend;
(Where late the sun did Atreus' crimes detest,
And disappear'd in horror of the feast).
And now by chance, by fate, or furies led,
From Bacchus' consecrated caves he fled,
Where the shrill cries of frantic matrons sound,
And Pentheus' blood enrich'd the rising ground;
Then sees Cithaeron towering o'er the plain,
And thence declining gently to the main;
Next to the bounds of Nisus' realm repairs,
Where treacherous Scylla cut the purple hairs;
The hanging cliffs of Scyron's rock explores,
And hears the murmurs of the different shores;
Passes the strait that parts the foaming seas,
And stately Corinth's pleasing site surveys.

'Twas now the time when Phoebus yields to night,
And rising Cynthia sheds her silver light;
Wide o'er the world in solemn pomp she drew
Her airy chariot, hung with pearly dew:
All birds and beasts lie hush'd; sleep steals away
The wild desires of men, and toils of day,
And brings, descending through the silent air,
A sweet forgetfulness of human care.
Yet no red clouds, with golden borders gay,
Promise the skies the bright return of day;
No faint reflections of the distant light
Streak with long gleams the scattering shades of night:
From the damp earth impervious vapours rise,
Increase the darkness, and involve the skies.
At once the rushing winds with roaring sound
Burst from th' Æolian caves, and rend the ground;
With equal rage their airy quarrel try,
And win by turns the kingdom of the sky;
But with a thicker night black Auster shrouds
The heavens, and drives on heaps the rolling clouds,

From whose dark womb a rattling tempest pours,
Which the cold north congeals to haily showers.
From pole to pole the thunder roars aloud,
And broken lightnings flash from every cloud.
Now smokes with showers the misty mountain-ground,
And floated fields lie undistinguish'd round;
Th' Inachian streams with headlong fury run,
And Erasinus rolls a deluge on;
The foaming Lerna swells above its bounds,
And spreads its ancient poisons o'er the grounds:
Where late was dust, now rapid torrents play,
Rush through the mounds, and bear the dams away:
Old limbs of trees, from crackling forests torn,
Are whirl'd in air, and on the winds are borne:
The storm the dark Lycæan groves display'd,
And first to light exposed the sacred shade.
Th' intrepid Theban hears the bursting sky,
Sees yawning rocks in massy fragments fly,
And views astonish'd, from the hills afar,
The floods descending, and the watery war,
That, driven by storms, and pouring o'er the plain,
Swept herds, and hinds, and houses to the main.
Through the brown horrors of the night he fled,
Nor knows, amazed, what doubtful path to tread;
His brother's image to his mind appears,
Inflames his heart with rage, and wings his feet with fears.

So fares the sailor on the stormy main,
When clouds conceal Bootes' golden wain,
When not a star its friendly lustre keeps,
Nor trembling Cynthia glimmers on the deeps;
He dreads the rocks, and shoals, and seas, and skies,
While thunder roars, and lightning round him flies.

Thus strove the chief, on every side distress'd;
Thus still his courage with his toils increased:
With his broad shield opposed, he forced his way
Through thickest woods, and roused the beasts of prey
Till he beheld, where from Larissa's height,
The shelving walls reflect a glancing light:
Thither with haste the Theban hero flies;
On this side Lerna's poisonous water lies,
On that Prosymna's grove and temple rise:
He pass'd the gates which then unguarded lay,
And to the regal palace bent his way;
On the cold marble, spent with toil, he lies,
And waits till pleasing slumbers seal his eyes.

Adrastus here his happy people sways,
Bless'd with calm peace in his declining days;
By both his parents of descent divine,
Great Jove and Phoebus graced his noble line:
Heaven had not crown'd his wishes with a son,
But two fair daughters heir'd his state and throne.
To him Apollo (wondrous to relate!
But who can pierce into the depths of fate?)
Had sung—'Expect thy sons on Argos' shore,
A yellow lion and a bristly boar.'
This, long revolved in his paternal breast,
Sat heavy on his heart, and broke his rest;
This, great Amphiaraus! lay hid from thee,
Though skill'd in fate and dark futurity.
The father's care and prophet's art were vain,
For thus did the predicting god ordain.

Lo, hapless Tydeus, whose ill-fated hand
Had slain his brother, leaves his native land,
And, seized with horror, in the shades of night,
Through the thick deserts headlong urged his flight:
Now by the fury of the tempest driven,
He seeks a shelter from th' inclement heaven,
Till, led by fate, the Theban's steps he treads,
And to fair Argos' open court succeeds.

When thus the chiefs from different lands resort
To Adrastus' realms and hospitable court,
The king surveys his guests with curious eyes,
And views their arms and habit with surprise.
A lion's yellow skin the Theban wears,
Horrid his mane, and rough with curling hairs:
Such once employ'd Alcides' youthful toils,
Ere yet adorn'd with Nemea's dreadful spoils.
A boar's stiff hide, of Calydonian breed,
Oenides' manly shoulders overspread;
Oblique his tusks, erect his bristles stood,
Alive, the pride and terror of the wood.

Struck with the sight, and fix'd in deep amaze,
The king th' accomplish'd oracle surveys,
Reveres Apollo's vocal caves, and owns
The guiding godhead, and his future sons.
O'er all his bosom secret transports reign,
And a glad horror shoots through every vein:
To heaven he lifts his hands, erects his sight,
And thus invokes the silent queen of night:

'Goddess of shades! beneath whose gloomy reign
Yon spangled arch glows with the starry train;
You who the cares of heaven and earth allay
Till nature, quicken'd by th' inspiring ray,
Wakes to new vigour with the rising day:
O thou who freest me from my doubtful state,
Long lost and wilder'd in the maze of fate,
Be present still, O goddess! in our aid;
Proceed, and firm those omens thou hast made.
We to thy name our annual rites will pay,
And on thy altars sacrifices lay;
The sable flock shall fall beneath the stroke,
And fill thy temples with a grateful smoke.
Hail, faithful Tripos! hail, ye dark abodes
Of awful Phoebus; I confess the gods!'

Thus, seized with sacred fear, the monarch pray'd;
Then to his inner court the guests convey'd,
Where yet thin fumes from dying sparks arise,
And dust yet white upon each altar lies,
The relics of a former sacrifice.
The king once more the solemn rites requires,
And bids renew the feasts and wake the fires.
His train obey; while all the courts around
With noisy care and various tumult sound.
Embroider'd purple clothes the golden beds;
This slave the floor, and that the table spreads;
A third dispels the darkness of the night,
And fills depending lamps with beams of light;
Here loaves in canisters are piled on high,
And there in flames the slaughter'd victims fly.
Sublime in regal state Adrastus shone,
Stretch'd on rich carpets on his ivory throne;
A lofty couch receives each princely guest;
Around, at awful distance, wait the rest.

And now the king, his royal feast to grace,
Acestis calls, the guardian of his race,
Who first their youth in arts of virtue train'd,
And their ripe years in modest grace maintain'd;
Then softly whisper'd in her faithful ear,
And bade his daughters at the rites appear.
When from the close apartments of the night
The royal nymphs approach, divinely bright,
Such was Diana's, such Minerva's face;
Nor shine their beauties with superior grace,
But that in these a milder charm endears,
And less of terror in their looks appears.

As on the heroes first they cast their eyes,
O'er their fair cheeks the glowing blushes rise;
Their downcast looks a decent shame confess'd,
Then on their father's reverend features rest.

The banquet done, the monarch gives the sign
To fill the goblet high with sparkling wine,
Which Danaus used in sacred rites of old,
With sculpture graced, and rough with rising gold:
Here to the clouds victorious Perseus flies,
Medusa seems to move her languid eyes,
And, e'en in gold, turns paler as she dies:
There from the chase Jove's towering eagle bears,
On golden wings, the Phrygian to the stars;
Still as he rises in th' ethereal height,
His native mountains lessen to his sight,
While all his sad companions upward gaze,
Fix'd on the glorious scene in wild amaze;
And the swift hounds, affrighted as he flies,
Run to the shade, and bark against the skies.

This golden bowl with generous juice was crown'd,
The first libation sprinkled on the ground;
By turns on each celestial power they call;
With Phoebus' name resounds the vaulted hall.
The courtly train, the strangers, and the rest,
Crown'd with chaste laurel, and with garlands dress'd,
While with rich gums the fuming altars blaze,
Salute the god in numerous hymns of praise.

Then thus the king: 'Perhaps, my noble guests,
These honour'd altars, and these annual feasts
To bright Apollo's awful name design'd,
Unknown, with wonder may perplex your mind.
Great was the cause: our old solemnities
From no blind zeal or fond tradition rise;
But saved from death, our Argives yearly pay
These grateful honours to the god of day.

'When by a thousand darts the Python slain,
With orbs unroll'd lay covering all the plain,
(Transfix'd as o'er Castalia's streams he hung,
And suck'd new poisons with his triple tongue),
To Argos' realms the victor god resorts,
And enters old Crotopus' humble courts.
This rural prince one only daughter bless'd,
That all the charms of blooming youth possess'd;
Pair was her face, and spotless was her mind,

Where filial love with virgin sweetness join'd:
Happy! and happy still she might have proved,
Were she less beautiful, or less beloved!
But Phoebus loved, and on the flowery side
Of Nemea's stream the yielding fair enjoy'd.
Now, ere ten moons their orb with light adorn,
Th' illustrious offspring of the god was born;
The nymph, her father's anger to evade,
Retires from Argos to the sylvan shade;
To woods and wilds the pleasing burden bears,
And trusts her infant to a shepherd's cares.

'How mean a fate, unhappy child! is thine!
Ah! how unworthy those of race divine!
On flowery herbs in some green covert laid,
His bed the ground, his canopy the shade,
He mixes with the bleating lambs his cries,
While the rude swain his rural music tries,
To call soft slumbers on his infant eyes.
Yet ev'n in those obscure abodes to live
Was more, alas! than cruel fate would give;
For on the grassy verdure as he lay,
And breathed the freshness of the early day,
Devouring dogs the helpless infant tore,
Fed on his trembling limbs, and lapp'd the gore.
Th' astonish'd mother, when the rumour came,
Forgets her father, and neglects her fame;
With loud complaints she fills the yielding air,
And beats her breast, and rends her flowing hair;
Then, wild with anguish, to her sire she flies,
Demands the sentence, and contented dies.

'But, touch'd with sorrow for the deed too late,
The raging god prepares t' avenge her fate.
He sends a monster horrible and fell,
Begot by Furies in the depths of hell.
The pest a virgin's face and bosom bears;
High on her crown a rising snake appears,
Guards her black front, and hisses in her hairs:
About the realm she walks her dreadful round,
When Night with sable wings o'erspreads the ground,
Devours young babes before their parents' eyes,
And feeds and thrives on public miseries.

'But generous rage the bold Choroebus warms,
Choroebus, famed for virtue as for arms.
Some few like him, inspired with martial flame,
Thought a short life well lost for endless fame.

These, where two ways in equal parts divide,
The direful monster from afar descried,
Two bleeding babes depending at her side,
Whose panting vitals, warm with life, she draws,
And in their hearts imbrues her cruel claws.
The youths surround her with extended spears;
But brave Choroebus in the front appears;
Deep in her breast he plunged his shining sword,
And hell's dire monster back to hell restored.
Th' Inachians view the slain with vast surprise,
Her twisting volumes, and her rolling eyes,
Her spotted breast, and gaping womb, imbrued
With livid poison and our children's blood.
The crowd in stupid wonder fix'd appear,
Pale ev'n in joy, nor yet forget to fear.
Some with vast beams the squalid corse engage,
And weary all the wild efforts of rage.
The birds obscene, that nightly flock'd to taste,
With hollow screeches fled the dire repast;
And ravenous dogs, allured by scented blood,
And starving wolves, ran howling to the wood.

'But fired with rage, from cleft Parnassus' brow
Avenging Phoebus bent his deadly bow,
And hissing flew the feather'd fates below:
A night of sultry clouds involved around
The towers, the fields, and the devoted ground:
And now a thousand lives together fled;
Death with his scythe cut off the fatal thread,
And a whole province in his triumph led.

'But Phoebus, ask'd why noxious fires appear,
And raging Sirius blasts the sickly year,
Demands their lives by whom his monster fell,
And dooms a dreadful sacrifice to hell.

'Bless'd be thy dust, and let eternal fame
Attend thy manes, and preserve thy name,
Undaunted hero! who, divinely brave,
In such a cause disdained thy life to save,
But view'd the shrine with a superior look,
And its upbraided godhead thus bespoke:
"With piety, the soul's securest guard,
And conscious virtue, still its own reward,
Willing I come, unknowing how to fear,
Nor shalt thou, Phoebus, find a suppliant here:
Thy monster's death to me was owed alone,
And 'tis a deed too glorious to disown.

Behold him here, for whom, so many days,
Impervious clouds conceal'd thy sullen rays;
For whom, as man no longer claim'd thy care,
Such numbers fell by pestilential air!
But if th' abandon'd race of human kind
From gods above no more compassion find;
If such inclemency in heaven can dwell,
Yet why must unoffending Argos feel
The vengeance due to this unlucky steel?
On me, on me, let all thy fury fall,
Nor err from me, since I deserve it all:
Unless our desert cities please thy sight,
Or funeral flames reflect a grateful light.
Discharge thy shafts, this ready bosom rend,
And to the shades a ghost triumphant send;
But for my country let my fate atone;
Be mine the vengeance, as the crime my own!"

'Merit distress'd, impartial heaven relieves:
Unwelcome life relenting Phoebus gives;
For not the vengeful power, that glow'd with rage,
With such amazing virtue durst engage.
The clouds dispersed, Apollo's wrath expired,
And from the wondering god th' unwilling youth retired.
Thence we these altars in his temple raise,
And offer annual honours, feasts, and praise;
These solemn feasts propitious Phoebus please;
These honours, still renew'd, his ancient wrath appease.

'But say, illustrious guest, (adjoin'd the king)
What name you bear, from what high race you spring?
The noble Tydeus stands confess'd, and known
Our neighbour prince, and heir of Calydon:
Relate your fortunes, while the friendly night
And silent hours to various talk invite.'

The Theban bends on earth his gloomy eyes,
Confused, and sadly thus at length replies:—
'Before these altars how shall I proclaim
(O generous prince!) my nation or my name,
Or through what veins our ancient blood has roll'd?
Let the sad tale for ever rest untold!
Yet if, propitious to a wretch unknown,
You seek to share in sorrows not your own,
Know then from Cadmus I derive my race,
Jocasta's son, and Thebes my native place.'

To whom the king (who felt his generous breast

Touch'd with concern for his unhappy guest)
Replies—'Ah! why forbears the son to name
His wretched father, known too well by fame?
Fame, that delights around the world to stray,
Scorns not to take our Argos in her way.
Ev'n those who dwell where suns at distance roll,
In northern wilds, and freeze beneath the pole,
And those who tread the burning Libyan lands,
The faithless Syrtes, and the moving sands;
Who view the western sea's extremest bounds,
Or drink of Ganges in their eastern grounds;
All these the woes of Oedipus have known,
Your fates, your furies, and your haunted town.
If on the sons the parents' crimes descend,
What prince from those his lineage can defend?
Be this thy comfort, that 'tis thine t' efface,
With virtuous acts, thy ancestors' disgrace,
And be thyself the honour of thy race.
But see! the stars begin to steal away,
And shine more faintly at approaching day;
Now pour the wine; and in your tuneful lays
Once more resound the great Apollo's praise.'

'O father Phoebus! whether Lycia's coast
And snowy mountains thy bright presence boast:
Whether to sweet Castalia thou repair,
And bathe in silver dews thy yellow hair;
Or pleased to find fair Delos float no more,
Delight in Cynthus and the shady shore;
Or choose thy seat in Ilion's proud abodes,
The shining structures raised by labouring gods:
By thee the bow and mortal shafts are borne;
Eternal charms thy blooming youth adorn:
Skill'd in the laws of secret fate above,
And the dark counsels of almighty Jove,
'Tis thine the seeds of future war to know,
The change of sceptres and impending woe,
When direful meteors spread through glowing air
Long trails of light and shake their blazing hair.
Thy rage the Phrygian felt, who durst aspire
T' excel the music of thy heavenly lyre;
Thy shafts avenged lewd Tityus' guilty flame,
Th' immortal victim of thy mother's fame;
Thy hand slew Python, and the dame who lost
Her numerous offspring for a fatal boast.
In Phlegyas' doom thy just revenge appears,
Condemn'd to Furies and eternal fears;
He views his food, but dreads, with lifted eye,

The mouldering rock that trembles from on high.

'Propitious hear our prayer, O power divine!
And on thy hospitable Argos shine;
Whether the style of Titan please thee more,
Whose purple rays th' Achæmenes adore:
Or great Osiris, who first taught the swain
In Pharian fields to sow the golden grain;
Or Mithra, to whose beams the Persian bows,
And pays, in hollow rocks, his awful vows;
Mithra! whose head the blaze of light adorns,
Who grasps the struggling heifer's lunar horns.'

JANUARY AND MAY.

FROM CHAUCER.

There lived in Lombardy, as authors write,
In days of old, a wise and worthy knight;
Of gentle manners, as of generous race,
Bless'd with much sense, more riches, and some grace:
Yet, led astray by Venus' soft delights,
He scarce could rule some idle appetites:
For long ago, let priests say what they could,
Weak sinful laymen were but flesh and blood.

But in due time, when sixty years were o'er,
He vow'd to lead this vicious life no more;
Whether pure holiness inspired his mind,
Or dotage turn'd his brain, is hard to find;
But his high courage prick'd him forth to wed,
And try the pleasures of a lawful bed.
This was his nightly dream, his daily care,
And to the heavenly powers his constant prayer,
Once, ere he died, to taste the blissful life
Of a kind husband and a loving wife.

These thoughts he fortified with reasons still
(For none want reasons to confirm their will).
Grave authors say, and witty poets sing,
That honest wedlock is a glorious thing:
But depth of judgment most in him appears
Who wisely weds in his maturer years.
Then let him choose a damsel young and fair,
To bless his age, and bring a worthy heir;
To soothe his cares, and, free from noise and strife,

Conduct him gently to the verge of life.
Let sinful bachelors their woes deplore,
Full well they merit all they feel, and more:
Unawed by precepts, human or divine,
Like birds and beasts, promiscuously they join;
Nor know to make the present blessing last,
To hope the future, or esteem the past:
But vainly boast the joys they never tried,
And find divulged the secrets they would hide.
The married man may bear his yoke with ease,
Secure at once himself and Heaven to please;
And pass his inoffensive hours away,
In bliss all night, and innocence all day:
Though fortune change, his constant spouse remains,
Augments his joys, or mitigates his pains.

But what so pure which envious tongues will spare?
Some wicked wits have libell'd all the fair.
With matchless impudence they style a wife
The dear-bought curse, and lawful plague of life;
A bosom serpent, a domestic evil,
A night invasion, and a midday devil.
Let not the wise these slanderous words regard,
But curse the bones of every lying bard.
All other goods by fortune's hand are given,
A wife is the peculiar gift of Heaven.
Vain fortune's favours, never at a stay,
Like empty shadows, pass, and glide away;
One solid comfort, our eternal wife,
Abundantly supplies us all our life:
This blessing lasts (if those who try say true)
As long as heart can wish—and longer too.

Our grandsire Adam, ere of Eve possess'd,
Alone, and e'en in Paradise unbless'd,
With mournful looks the blissful scenes survey'd,
And wander'd in the solitary shade.
The Maker saw, took pity, and bestow'd
Woman, the last, the best reserved of God.

A wife! ah, gentle deities! can he
That has a wife e'er feel adversity?
Would men but follow what the sex advise,
All things would prosper, all the world grow wise.
Twas by Rebecca's aid that Jacob won
His father's blessing from an elder son:
Abusive Nabal owed his forfeit life
To the wise conduct of a prudent wife:

Heroic Judith, as old Hebrews show,
Preserved the Jews, and slew th' Assyrian foe:
At Hester's suit, the persecuting sword
Was sheath'd, and Israel lived to bless the Lord.

These weighty motives January the sage
Maturely ponder'd in his riper age;
And, charm'd with virtuous joys, and sober life,
Would try that Christian comfort, call'd a wife.
His friends were summon'd on a point so nice
To pass their judgment, and to give advice;
But fix'd before, and well resolved was he;
(As men that ask advice are wont to be).

'My friends,' he cried (and cast a mournful look
Around the room, and sigh'd before he spoke),
'Beneath the weight of threescore years I bend,
And, worn with cares, am hastening to my end:
How I have lived, alas! you know too well,
In worldly follies which I blush to tell,
But gracious Heaven has oped my eyes at last,
With due regret I view my vices past,
And, as the precept of the church decrees,
Will take a wife, and live in holy ease:
But since by counsel all things should be done,
And many heads are wiser still than one;
Choose you for me, who best shall be content
When my desire's approved by your consent.

'One caution yet is needful to be told,
To guide your choice: this wife must not be old:
There goes a saying, and 'twas shrewdly said,
Old fish at table, but young flesh in bed.
My soul abhors the tasteless dry embrace
Of a stale virgin with a winter face:
In that cold season Love but treats his guest
With beanstraw, and tough forage at the best.
No crafty widows shall approach my bed;
Those are too wise for bachelors to wed.
As subtle clerks by many schools are made,
Twice-married dames are mistresses o' th' trade:
But young and tender virgins, ruled with ease,
We form like wax, and mould them as we please.

'Conceive me, sirs, nor take my sense amiss;
'Tis what concerns my soul's eternal bliss;
Since, if I found no pleasure in my spouse,
As flesh is frail, and who (God help me) knows?

Then should I live in lewd adultery,
And sink downright to Satan when I die:
Or were I cursed with an unfruitful bed,
The righteous end were lost for which I wed;
To raise up seed to bless the powers above,
And not for pleasure only, or for love.
Think not I dote; 'tis time to take a wife,
When vigorous blood forbids a chaster life:
Those that are bless'd with store of grace divine,
May live like saints, by Heaven's consent and mine!

'And since I speak of wedlock, let me say
(As, thank my stars, in modest truth I may),
My limbs are active, still I'm sound at heart,
And a new vigour springs in every part.
Think not my virtue lost, though time has shed
These reverend honours on my hoary head:
Thus trees are crown'd with blossoms white as snow,
The vital sap then rising from below.
Old as I am, my lusty limbs appear
Like winter greens, that flourish all the year.
Now, sirs, you know to what I stand inclined,
Let every friend with freedom speak his mind.'

He said; the rest in different parts divide;
The knotty point was urged on either side:
Marriage, the theme on which they all declaim'd,
Some praised with wit, and some with reason blamed.
Till, what with proofs, objections, and replies,
Each wondrous positive and wondrous wise,
There fell between his brothers a debate:
Placebo this was call'd, and Justin that.

First to the knight Placebo thus begun,
(Mild were his looks, and pleasing was his tone):
'Such prudence, sir, in all your words appears,
As plainly proves experience dwells with years!
Yet you pursue sage Solomon's advice,
To work by counsel when affairs are nice:
But, with the wise man's leave, I must protest,
So may my soul arrive at ease and rest,
As still I hold your own advice the best.

'Sir, I have lived a courtier all my days,
And studied men, their manners, and their ways;
And have observed this useful maxim still.
To let my betters always have their will.
Nay, if my lord affirm'd that black was white,

My word was this, "Your honour's in the right."
Th' assuming wit, who deems himself so wise
As his mistaken patron to advise,
Let him not dare to vent his dangerous thought;
A noble fool was never in a fault.
This, sir, affects not you, whose every word
Is weigh'd with judgment, and befits a lord:
Your will is mine: and is (I will maintain)
Pleasing to God, and should be so to man;
At least your courage all the world must praise,
Who dare to wed in your declining days.
Indulge the vigour of your mounting blood,
And let gray fools be indolently good,
Who, past all pleasure, damn the joys of sense,
With reverend dulness and grave impotence.'

Justin, who silent sate, and heard the man,
Thus with a philosophic frown began:

'A heathen author, of the first degree,
(Who, though not faith, had sense as well as we),
Bids us be certain our concerns to trust
To those of generous principles and just.
The venture's greater, I'll presume to say,
To give your person, than your goods away:
And therefore, sir, as you regard your rest,
First learn your lady's qualities at least:
Whether she's chaste or rampant, proud or civil,
Meek as a saint, or haughty as the devil;
Whether an easy, fond, familiar fool,
Or such a wit as no man e'er can rule.
'Tis true, perfection none must hope to find
In all this world, much less in womankind:
But if her virtues prove the larger share,
Bless the kind fates, and think your fortune rare.
Ah, gentle sir, take warning of a friend,
Who knows too well the state you thus commend;
And, spite of all his praises, must declare,
All he can find is bondage, cost, and care.
Heaven knows I shed full many a private tear,
And sigh in silence, lest the world should hear;
While all my friends applaud my blissful life,
And swear no mortal's happier in a wife;
Demure and chaste as any vestal nun,
The meekest creature that beholds the sun!
But, by th' immortal powers, I feel the pain,
And he that smarts has reason to complain.
Do what you list, for me; you must be sage,

And cautious sure; for wisdom is in age:
But at these years to venture on the fair!
By Him who made the ocean, earth, and air,
To please a wife, when her occasions call,
Would busy the most vigorous of us all.
And trust me, sir, the chastest you can choose,
Will ask observance, and exact her dues.
If what I speak my noble lord offend,
My tedious sermon here is at an end.'

''Tis well, 'tis wondrous well,' the knight replies,
'Most worthy kinsman, faith, you're mighty wise!
We, sirs, are fools; and must resign the cause
To heathenish authors, proverbs, and old saws.'
He spoke with scorn, and turn'd another way:
'What does my friend, my dear Placebo, say?'

'I say,' quoth he, 'by Heaven, the man's to blame,
To slander wives, and wedlock's holy name.'

At this the council rose without delay;
Each, in his own opinion, went his way;
With full consent, that, all disputes appeased,
The knight should marry when and where he pleased.

Who now but January exults with joy?
The charms of wedlock all his soul employ:
Each nymph by turns his wavering mind possess'd,
And reign'd the short-lived tyrant of his breast;
Whilst fancy pictured every lively part,
And each bright image wander'd o'er his heart.
Thus, in some public forum fix'd on high,
A mirror shows the figures moving by;
Still one by one, in swift succession, pass
The gliding shadows o'er the polish'd glass.
This lady's charms the nicest could not blame,
But vile suspicions had aspersed her fame;
That was with sense, but not with virtue bless'd;
And one had grace that wanted all the rest.
Thus doubting long what nymph he should obey
He fix'd at last upon the youthful May.
Her faults he knew not, love is always blind,
But every charm revolved within his mind:
Her tender age, her form divinely fair,
Her easy motion, her attractive air,
Her sweet behaviour, her enchanting face,
Her moving softness, and majestic grace.
Much in his prudence did our knight rejoice,

And thought no mortal could dispute his choice:
Once more in haste he summon'd every friend,
And told them all their pains were at an end.
'Heaven, that (said he) inspired me first to wed,
Provides a consort worthy of my bed:
Let none oppose th' election, since on this
Depends my quiet and my future bliss.

'A dame there is, the darling of my eyes,
Young, beauteous, artless, innocent, and wise;
Chaste, though not rich; and, though not nobly born,
Of honest parents, and may serve my turn.
Her will I wed, if gracious Heaven so please,
To pass my age in sanctity and ease;
And, thank the powers, I may possess alone
The lovely prize, and share my bliss with none!
If you, my friends, this virgin can procure,
My joys are full, my happiness is sure.

'One only doubt remains: full oft, I've heard
By casuists grave, and deep divines averr'd,
That 'tis too much for human race to know
The bliss of heaven above and earth below;
Now, should the nuptial pleasures prove so great,
To match the blessings of the future state,
Those endless joys were ill exchanged for these;
Then clear this doubt, and set my mind at ease.'

This Justin heard, nor could his spleen control,
Touch'd to the quick, and tickled at the soul.
'Sir knight,' he cried, 'if this be all you dread,
Heaven put it past your doubt whene'er you wed:
And to my fervent prayers so far consent,
That, ere the rites are o'er, you may repent!
Good Heaven, no doubt, the nuptial state approves,
Since it chastises still what best it loves.
Then be not, sir, abandoned to despair:
Seek, and perhaps you'll find among the fair
One that may do your business to a hair;
Not e'en in wish your happiness delay,
But prove the scourge to lash you on your way:
Then to the skies your mounting soul shall go,
Swift as an arrow soaring from the bow!
Provided still, you moderate your joy,
Nor in your pleasures all your might employ;
Let reason's rule your strong desires abate,
Nor please too lavishly your gentle mate
Old wives there are, of judgment most acute,

Who solve these questions beyond all dispute;
Consult with those, and be of better cheer;
Marry, do penance, and dismiss your fear.'

So said, they rose, nor more the work delay'd
The match was offer'd, the proposals made.
The parents, you may think, would soon comply
The old have interest ever in their eye.
Nor was it hard to move the lady's mind;
When fortune favours, still the fair are kind.

I pass each previous settlement and deed,
Too long for me to write, or you to read;
Nor will with quaint impertinence display
The pomp, the pageantry, the proud array.
The time approach'd; to church the parties went,
At once with carnal and devout intent:
Forth came the priest, and bade the obedient wife
Like Sarah or Rebecca lead her life;
Then pray'd the powers the fruitful bed to bless,
And made all sure enough with holiness.

And now the palace gates are open'd wide,
The guests appear in order, side by side,
And, placed in state, the bridegroom and the bride.
The breathing flute's soft notes are heard around,
And the shrill trumpets mix their silver sound;
The vaulted roofs with echoing music ring,
These touch the vocal stops, and those the trembling string.
Not thus Amphion tuned the warbling lyre,
Nor Joab the sounding clarion could inspire,
Nor fierce Theodamas, whose sprightly strain
Could swell the soul to rage, and fire the martial train.

Bacchus himself, the nuptial feast to grace,
(So poets sing) was present on the place:
And lovely Venus, goddess of delight,
Shook high her flaming torch in open sight,
And danced around, and smiled on every knight:
Pleased her best servant would his courage try,
No less in wedlock than in liberty.
Full many an age old Hymen had not spied
So kind a bridegroom, or so bright a bride.
Ye bards! renown'd among the tuneful throng
For gentle lays, and joyous nuptial song,
Think not your softest numbers can display
The matchless glories of this blissful day;
The joys are such as far transcend your rage,

When tender youth has wedded stooping age.

The beauteous dame sat smiling at the board,
And darted amorous glances at her lord.
Not Hester's self, whose charms the Hebrews sing,
E'er look'd so lovely on her Persian king:
Bright as the rising sun in summer's day,
And fresh and blooming as the month of May!
The joyful knight survey'd her by his side,
Nor envied Paris with his Spartan bride:
Still as his mind revolved with vast delight
Th' entrancing raptures of th' approaching night,
Restless he sat, invoking every power
To speed his bliss, and haste the happy hour.
Meantime the vigorous dancers beat the ground,
And songs were sung, and flowing bowls went round.
With odorous spices they perfumed the place,
And mirth and pleasure shone in every face.

Damian alone, of all the menial train,
Sad in the midst of triumphs, sigh'd for pain;
Damian alone, the knight's obsequious squire,
Consumed at heart, and fed a secret fire.
His lovely mistress all his soul possess'd,
He look'd, he languish'd, and could take no rest:
His task perform'd, he sadly went his way,
Fell on his bed, and loath'd the light of day:
There let him lie; till his relenting dame
Weep in her turn, and waste in equal flame.

The weary sun, as learnèd poets write,
Forsook th' horizon, and roll'd down the light;
While glittering stars his absent beams supply.
And night's dark mantle overspread the sky.
Then rose the guests, and, as the time required,
Each paid his thanks, and decently retired.

The foe once gone, our knight prepared t' undress,
So keen he was, and eager to possess;
But first thought fit th' assistance to receive,
Which grave physicians scruple not to give:
Satyrion near, with hot eringoes stood,
Cantharides, to fire the lazy blood,
Whose use old bards describe in luscious rhymes,
And critics learn'd explain to modern times.

By this the sheets were spread, the bride undress'd,
The room was sprinkled, and the bed was bless'd.

What next ensued beseems not me to say;
'Tis sung, he labour'd till the dawning day,
Then briskly sprung from bed, with heart so light,
As all were nothing he had done by night,
And sipp'd his cordial as he sat upright.
He kiss'd his balmy spouse with wanton play,
And feebly sung a lusty roundelay:
Then on the couch his weary limbs he cast;
For every labour must have rest at last.

But anxious cares the pensive squire oppress'd,
Sleep fled his eyes, and peace forsook his breast;
The raging flames that in his bosom dwell,
He wanted art to hide, and means to tell:
Yet hoping time th' occasion might betray,
Composed a sonnet to the lovely May;
Which, writ and folded with the nicest art,
He wrapp'd in silk, and laid upon his heart.

When now the fourth revolving day was run,
('Twas June, and Cancer had received the sun),
Forth from her chamber came the beauteous bride;
The good old knight moved slowly by her side.
High mass was sung; they feasted in the hall;
The servants round stood ready at their call
The squire alone was absent from the board,
And much his sickness grieved his worthy lord,
Who pray'd his spouse, attended with her train,
To visit Damian, and divert his pain.
Th' obliging dames obey'd with one consent:
They left the hall, and to his lodging went.
The female tribe surround him as he lay,
And close beside him sat the gentle May:
Where, as she tried his pulse, he softly drew
A heaving sigh, and cast a mournful view!
Then gave his bill, and bribed the Powers divine
With secret vows, to favour his design.

Who studies now but discontented May?
On her soft couch uneasily she lay:
The lumpish husband snored away the night,
Till coughs awaked him near the morning light.
What then he did, I'll not presume to tell,
Nor if she thought herself in heaven or hell:
Honest and dull in nuptial bed they lay,
Till the bell toll'd, and all arose to pray.

Were it by forceful destiny decreed,

Or did from chance, or nature's power proceed;
Or that some star, with aspect kind to love,
Shed its selectest influence from above;
Whatever was the cause, the tender dame
Felt the first motions of an infant flame;
Received th' impressions of the love-sick squire,
And wasted in the soft infectious fire.

Ye fair, draw near, let May's example move
Your gentle minds to pity those who love!
Had some fierce tyrant in her stead been found,
The poor adorer sure had hang'd or drown'd;
But she, your sex's mirror, free from pride,
Was much too meek to prove a homicide.

But to my tale:—Some sages have defined
Pleasure the sovereign bliss of humankind:
Our knight (who studied much, we may suppose)
Derived his high philosophy from those;
For, like a prince, he bore the vast expense
Of lavish pomp, and proud magnificence:
His house was stately, his retinue gay,
Large was his train, and gorgeous his array.
His spacious garden, made to yield to none,
Was compass'd round with walls of solid stone;
Priapus could not half describe the grace
(Though god of gardens) of this charming place:
A place to tire the rambling wits of France
In long descriptions, and exceed romance:
Enough to shame the gentlest bard that sings
Of painted meadows, and of purling springs.

Full in the centre of the flowery ground
A crystal fountain spread its streams around,
The fruitful banks with verdant laurels crown'd.
About this spring (if ancient fame say true)
The dapper elves their moonlight sports pursue:
Their pigmy king, and little fairy queen,
In circling dances gamboll'd on the green,
While tuneful sprites a merry concert made,
And airy music warbled through the shade.

Hither the noble knight would oft repair,
(His scene of pleasure, and peculiar care):
For this he held it dear, and always bore
The silver key that lock'd the garden door.
To this sweet place, in summer's sultry heat,
He used from noise and business to retreat:

And here in dalliance spend the livelong day,
Solus cum sola, with his sprightly May:
For whate'er work was undischarged abed,
The duteous knight in this fair garden sped.

But ah! what mortal lives of bliss secure?
How short a space our worldly joys endure!
O Fortune! fair, like all thy treacherous kind,
But faithless still, and wavering as the wind!
O painted monster, form'd mankind to cheat
With pleasing poison, and with soft deceit!
This rich, this amorous, venerable knight,
Amidst his ease, his solace, and delight,
Struck blind by thee, resigns his days to grief,
And calls on death, the wretch's last relief.

The rage of jealousy then seized his mind,
For much he fear'd the faith of womankind.
His wife, not suffer'd from his side to stray,
Was captive kept; he watch'd her night and day,
Abridged her pleasures, and confined her sway.
Full oft in tears did hapless May complain,
And sigh'd full oft; but sigh'd and wept in vain:
She look'd on Damian with a lover's eye;
For oh, 'twas fix'd; she must possess or die!
Nor less impatience vex'd her amorous squire,
Wild with delay, and burning with desire.
Watch'd as she was, yet could he not refrain
By secret writing to disclose his pain;
The dame by signs reveal'd her kind intent,
Till both were conscious what each other meant.

Ah! gentle knight, what would thy eyes avail,
Though they could see as far as ships can sail?
'Tis better, sure, when blind, deceived to be,
Than be deluded when a man can see!

Argus himself, so cautious and so wise,
Was overwatch'd, for all his hundred eyes:
So many an honest husband may, 'tis known,
Who, wisely, never thinks the case his own.

The dame at last, by diligence and care,
Procured the key her knight was wont to bear;
She took the wards in wax before the fire,
And gave th' impression to the trusty squire.
By means of this some wonder shall appear,
Which, in due place and season, you may hear.

Well sung sweet Ovid, in the days of yore,
What slight is that which love will not explore?
And Pyramus and Thisbe plainly show
The feats true lovers, when they list, can do:
Though watch'd and captive, yet in spite of all,
They found the art of kissing through a wall.

But now no longer from our tale to stray;
It happ'd, that once, upon a summer's day,
Our reverend knight was urged to amorous play;
He raised his spouse ere matin-bell was rung,
And thus his morning canticle he sung:

'Awake, my love, disclose thy radiant eyes!
Arise, my wife, my beauteous lady, rise!
Hear how the doves with pensive notes complain,
And in soft murmurs tell the trees their pain:
The winter's past; the clouds and tempests fly;
The sun adorns the fields, and brightens all the sky.
Fair without spot, whose every charming part
My bosom wounds, and captivates my heart!
Come, and in mutual pleasures let's engage,
Joy of my life, and comfort of my age!'

This heard, to Damian straight a sign she made
To haste before; the gentle squire obey'd:
Secret and undescried he took his way,
And, ambush'd close, behind an arbour lay.

It was not long ere January came,
And hand in hand with him his lovely dame;
Blind as he was, not doubting all was sure,
He turn'd the key, and made the gate secure.

'Here let us walk,' he said, 'observed by none,
Conscious of pleasures to the world unknown:
So may my soul have joy, as thou, my wife,
Art far the dearest solace of my life;
And rather would I choose, by heaven above!
To die this instant, than to lose thy love.
Reflect what truth was in my passion shown,
When, unendow'd, I took thee for my own,
And sought no treasure but thy heart alone.
Old as I am, and now deprived of sight,
Whilst thou art faithful to thy own true knight,
Nor age, nor blindness rob me of delight.
Each other loss with patience I can bear,
The loss of thee is what I only fear.

'Consider then, my lady, and my wife,
The solid comforts of a virtuous life.
As, first, the love of Christ himself you gain;
Next, your own honour undefiled maintain;
And, lastly, that which sure your mind must move,
My whole estate shall gratify your love:
Make your own terms, and ere to-morrow's sun
Displays his light, by heaven, it shall be done!
I seal the contract with a holy kiss,
And will perform, by this—my dear, and this—
Have comfort, spouse, nor think thy lord unkind;
'Tis love, not jealousy, that fires my mind!
For when thy charms my sober thoughts engage,
And join'd to them my own unequal age,
From thy dear side I have no power to part,
Such secret transports warm my melting heart.
For who that once possess'd those heavenly charms,
Could live one moment absent from thy arms?'

He ceased, and May with modest grace replied,
(Weak was her voice, as while she spoke she cried):
'Heaven knows (with that a tender sigh she drew)
I have a soul to save as well as you;
And, what no less you to my charge commend,
My dearest honour will to death defend.
To you in holy church I gave my hand,
And join'd my heart in wedlock's sacred band:
Yet after this, if you distrust my care,
Then hear, my lord, and witness what I swear:

'First may the yawning earth her bosom rend,
And let me hence to hell alive descend;
Or die the death I dread no less than hell,
Sew'd in a sack, and plunged into a well,
Ere I my fame by one lewd act disgrace,
Or once renounce the honour of my race.
For know, sir knight, of gentle blood I came;
I loathe a whore, and startle at the name.
But jealous men on their own crimes reflect,
And learn from thence their ladies to suspect:
Else why these heedless cautions, sir, to me
These doubts and fears of female constancy
This chime still rings in every lady's ear,
The only strain a wife must hope to hear.'

Thus while she spoke a sidelong glance she cast,
Where Damian, kneeling, worshipp'd as she pass'd.

She saw him watch the motions of her eye,
And singled out a pear-tree planted nigh:
'Twas charged with fruit that made a goodly show,
And hung with dangling pears was every bough.
Thither th' obsequious squire address'd his pace,
And, climbing, in the summit took his place;
The knight and lady walk'd beneath in view,
Where let us leave them and our tale pursue.

'Twas now the season when the glorious sun
His heavenly progress through the Twins had run;
And Jove, exalted, his mild influence yields,
To glad the glebe, and paint the flowery fields:
Clear was the day, and Phoebus, rising bright,
Had streak'd the azure firmament with light;
He pierced the glittering clouds with golden streams,
And warm'd the womb of earth with genial beams.

It so befell, in that fair morning tide,
The fairies sported on the garden side,
And in the midst their monarch and his bride.
So featly tripp'd the light-foot ladies round,
The knights so nimbly o'er the greensward bound,
That scarce they bent the flowers or touch'd the ground.
The dances ended, all the fairy train
For pinks and daisies search'd the flowery plain;
While on a bank reclined of rising green,
Thus, with a frown, the king bespoke his queen:

"Tis too apparent, argue what you can,
The treachery you women use to man:
A thousand authors have this truth made out,
And sad experience leaves no room for doubt.

'Heaven rest thy spirit, noble Solomon!
A wiser monarch never saw the sun:
All wealth, all honours, the supreme degree
Of earthly bliss, was well bestow'd on thee!
For sagely hast thou said, Of all mankind,
One only just, and righteous, hope to find:
But shouldst thou search the spacious world around,
Yet one good woman is not to be found.

'Thus says the king, who knew your wickedness;
The son of Sirach testifies no less.
So may some wild-fire on your bodies fall,
Or some devouring plague consume you all;
As well you view the lecher in the tree,

And well this honourable knight you see:
But, since he's blind and old (a helpless case),
His squire shall cuckold him before your face.

'Now by my own dread majesty I swear,
And by this awful sceptre which I bear,
No impious wretch shall 'scape unpunish'd long,
That in my presence offers such a wrong.
I will this instant undeceive the knight,
And in the very act restore his sight:
And set the strumpet here in open view,
A warning to these ladies, and to you,
And all the faithless sex, for ever to be true.'

'And will you so,' replied the queen, 'indeed?
Now, by my mother's soul, it is decreed,
She shall not want an answer at her need.
For her, and for her daughters, I'll engage,
And all the sex in each succeeding age;
Art shall be theirs to varnish an offence,
And fortify their crimes with confidence.
Nay, were they taken in a strict embrace,
Seen with both eyes, and pinion'd on the place;
All they shall need is to protest and swear,
Breathe a soft sigh, and drop a tender tear;
Till their wise husbands, gull'd by arts like these,
Grow gentle, tractable, and tame as geese.

'What though this slanderous Jew, this Solomon,
Call'd women fools, and knew full many a one;
The wiser wits of later times declare
How constant, chaste, and virtuous women are:
Witness the martyrs who resign'd their breath,
Serene in torments, unconcern'd in death;
And witness next what Roman authors tell,
How Arria, Portia, and Lucretia fell.

'But since the sacred leaves to all are free,
And men interpret texts, why should not we?
By this no more was meant than to have shown
That sovereign goodness dwells in Him alone,
Who only Is, and is but only One.
But grant the worst; shall women then be weigh'd
By every word that Solomon hath said
What though this king (as ancient story boasts)
Built a fair temple to the Lord of Hosts;
He ceased at last his Maker to adore,
And did as much for idol gods, or more.

Beware what lavish praises you confer
On a rank lecher and idolater;
Whose reign indulgent God, says Holy Writ,
Did but for David's righteous sake permit;
David the monarch after Heaven's own mind,
Who loved our sex, and honour'd all our kind.

'Well, I'm a woman, and as such must speak;
Silence would swell me, and my heart would break.
Know, then, I scorn your dull authorities,
Your idle wits, and all their learned lies:
By heaven, those authors are our sex's foes,
Whom, in our right, I must and will oppose!'

'Nay,' quoth the king, 'dear madam, be not wroth;
I yield it up; but since I gave my oath,
That this much-injured knight again should see;
It must be done—I am a king,' said he,
'And one whose faith has ever sacred been—'

'And so has mine' (she said)—'I am a queen:
Her answer she shall have, I undertake;
And thus an end of all dispute I make.
Try when you list; and you shall find, my lord,
It is not in our sex to break our word.'

We leave them here in this heroic strain,
And to the knight our story turns again;
Who in the garden, with his lovely May,
Sung merrier than the cuckoo or the jay:
This was his song, 'Oh kind and constant be;
Constant and kind I'll ever prove to thee.'

Thus singing as he went, at last he drew
By easy steps to where the pear-tree grew:
The longing dame look'd up, and spied her love
Full fairly perch'd among the boughs above.
She stopp'd, and sighing, 'O good gods!' she cried,
'What pangs, what sudden shoots distend my side
Oh for that tempting fruit, so fresh, so green;
Help, for the love of heaven's immortal queen!
Help, dearest lord, and save at once the life
Of thy poor infant, and thy longing wife!'

Sore sigh'd the knight to hear his lady's cry,
But could not climb, and had no servant nigh:
Old as he was, and void of eyesight too,
What could, alas! a helpless husband do?

'And must I languish, then, (she said), and die,
Yet view the lovely fruit before my eye?
At least, kind sir, for charity's sweet sake,
Vouchsafe the trunk between your arms to take;
Then from your back I might ascend the tree;
Do you but stoop, and leave the rest to me.'

'With all my soul,' he thus replied again,
'I'd spend my dearest blood to ease thy pain.'
With that his back against the trunk he bent;
She seized a twig, and up the tree she went.

Now prove your patience, gentle ladies all!
Nor let on me your heavy anger fall:
'Tis truth I tell, though not in phrase refined;
Though blunt my tale, yet honest is my mind.
What feats the lady in the tree might do,
I pass, as gambols never known to you;
But sure it was a merrier fit, she swore,
Than in her life she ever felt before.

In that nice moment, lo! the wondering knight
Look'd out, and stood restored to sudden sight.
Straight on the tree his eager eyes he bent,
As one whose thoughts were on his spouse intent;
But when he saw his bosom-wife so dress'd,
His rage was such as cannot be express'd:
Not frantic mothers, when their infants die,
With louder clamours rend the vaulted sky:
He cried, he roar'd, he storm'd, he tore his hair:
'Death! hell! and furies! what dost thou do there?'

'What ails my lord?' the trembling dame replied,
'I thought your patience had been better tried:
Is this your love, ungrateful and unkind,
This my reward for having cured the blind?
Why was I taught to make my husband see,
By struggling with a man upon a tree
Did I for this the power of magic prove?
Unhappy wife, whose crime was too much love!'

'If this be struggling, by this holy light,
'Tis struggling with a vengeance (quoth the knight):
So Heaven preserve the sight it has restored,
As with these eyes I plainly saw thee whored;
Whored by my slave—perfidious wretch! may hell
As surely seize thee, as I saw too well.'

'Guard me, good angels!' cried the gentle May,
'Pray heaven this magic work the proper way!
Alas, my love! 'tis certain, could you see,
You ne'er had used these killing words to me:
So help me, Fates! as 'tis no perfect sight,
But some faint glimmering of a doubtful light.'

'What I have said (quoth he) I must maintain,
For by th' immortal powers it seem'd too plain—'

'By all those powers, some frenzy seized your mind
(Replied the dame), are these the thanks I find?
Wretch that I am, that e'er I was so kind!'
She said; a rising sigh express'd her woe,
The ready tears apace began to flow,
And, as they fell, she wiped from either eye
The drops (for women, when they list, can cry).

The knight was touch'd; and in his looks appear'd
Signs of remorse, while thus his spouse he cheer'd:
'Madam, 'tis past, and my short anger o'er!
Come down, and vex your tender heart no more:
Excuse me, dear, if aught amiss was said,
For, on my soul, amends shall soon be made:
Let my repentance your forgiveness draw;
By heaven, I swore but what I thought I saw.'

'Ah, my loved lord! 'twas much unkind (she cried)
On bare suspicion thus to treat your bride.
But, till your sight's establish'd, for a while,
Imperfect objects may your sense beguile.
Thus, when from sleep we first our eyes display,
The balls are wounded with the piercing ray,
And dusky vapours rise and intercept the day;
So, just recovering from the shades of night,
Your swimming eyes are drunk with sudden light,
Strange phantoms dance around, and skim before your sight.
Then, sir, be cautious, nor too rashly deem;
Heaven knows how seldom things are what they seem!
Consult your reason, and you soon shall find
'Twas you were jealous, not your wife unkind:
Jove ne'er spoke oracle more true than this,
None judge so wrong as those who think amiss.'

With that she leap'd into her lord's embrace,
With well-dissembled virtue in her face.
He hugg'd her close, and kiss'd her o'er and o'er,
Disturb'd with doubts and jealousies no more:

Both, pleased and bless'd, renew'd their mutual vows:
A fruitful wife, and a believing spouse.

Thus ends our tale, whose moral next to make,
Let all wise husbands hence example take;
And pray, to crown the pleasure of their lives,
To be so well deluded by their wives.

THE WIFE OF BATH, HER PROLOGUE.

FROM CHAUCER.

Behold the woes of matrimonial life,
And hear with reverence an experienced wife!
To dear-bought wisdom give the credit due,
And think, for once, a woman tells you true.
In all these trials I have borne a part:
I was myself the scourge that caused the smart;
For, since fifteen, in triumph have I led
Five captive husbands from the church to bed.

Christ saw a wedding once, the Scripture says,
And saw but one, 'tis thought, in all his days;
Whence some infer, whose conscience is too nice,
No pious Christian ought to marry twice.

But let them read, and solve me if they can,
The words address'd to the Samaritan;
Five times in lawful wedlock she was join'd,
And sure the certain stint was ne'er defined.

'Increase and multiply' was Heaven's command,
And that's a text I clearly understand:
This, too, 'Let men their sires and mothers leave,
And to their dearer wives for ever cleave.'
More wives than one by Solomon were tried,
Or else the wisest of mankind's belied.
I've had myself full many a merry fit,
And trust in heaven I may have many yet;
For when my transitory spouse, unkind,
Shall die and leave his woful wife behind,
I'll take the next good Christian I can find.

Paul, knowing one could never serve our turn,
Declared 'twas better far to wed than burn.
There's danger in assembling fire and tow;

I grant 'em that; and what it means you know.
The same apostle, too, has elsewhere own'd
No precept for virginity he found:
'Tis but a counsel—and we women still
Take which we like, the counsel or our will.

I envy not their bliss, if he or she
Think fit to live in perfect chastity:
Pure let them be, and free from taint or vice;
I for a few slight spots am not so nice.
Heaven calls us different ways; on these bestows
One proper gift, another grants to those;
Not every man's obliged to sell his store,
And give up all his substance to the poor:
Such as are perfect may, I can't deny;
But, by your leaves, divines! so am not I.

Full many a saint, since first the world began,
Lived an unspotted maid in spite of man:
Let such (a God's name) with fine wheat be fed,
And let us honest wives eat barley bread.
For me, I'll keep the post assign'd by heaven,
And use the copious talent it has given:
Let my good spouse pay tribute, do me right,
And keep an equal reckoning every night;
His proper body is not his, but mine;
For so said Paul, and Paul's a sound divine.

Know then, of those five husbands I have had,
Three were just tolerable, two were bad.
The three were old, but rich and fond beside,
And toil'd most piteously to please their bride;
But since their wealth (the best they had) was mine,
The rest, without much loss, I could resign:
Sure to be loved, I took no pains to please,
Yet had more pleasure far than they had ease.

Presents flow'd in apace: with showers of gold
They made their court, like Jupiter of old:
If I but smiled, a sudden youth they found,
And a new palsy seized them when I frown'd.
Ye sovereign wives! give ear, and understand:
Thus shall ye speak, and exercise command;
For never was it given to mortal man
To lie so boldly as we women can:
Forswear the fact, though seen with both his eyes,
And call your maids to witness how he lies.

Hark, old Sir Paul! ('twas thus I used to say)
Whence is our neighbour's wife so rich and gay
Treated, caress'd, where'er she's pleased to roam—
I sit in tatters, and immured at home.
Why to her house dost thou so oft repair?
Art thou so amorous? and is she so fair?
If I but see a cousin or a friend,
Lord! how you swell and rage, like any fiend!
But you reel home, a drunken beastly bear,
Then preach till midnight in your easy chair;
Cry, Wives are false, and every woman evil,
And give up all that's female to the devil.
If poor (you say), she drains her husband's purse;
If rich, she keeps her priest, or something worse;
If highly born, intolerably vain,
Vapours and pride by turns possess her brain;
Now gaily mad, now sourly splenetic,
Freakish when well, and fretful when she's sick:
If fair, then chaste she cannot long abide,
By pressing youth attack'd on every side;
If foul, her wealth the lusty lover lures,
Or else her wit some fool-gallant procures,
Or else she dances with becoming grace,
Or shape excuses the defects of face.
There swims no goose so gray, but soon or late
She finds some honest gander for her mate.

Horses (thou say'st) and asses men may try,
And ring suspected vessels ere they buy;
But wives, a random choice, untried they take,
They dream in courtship, but in wedlock wake;
Then, nor till then, the veil's removed away,
And all the woman glares in open day.

You tell me, to preserve your wife's good grace,
Your eyes must always languish on my face,
Your tongue with constant flatteries feed my ear,
And tag each sentence with 'My life! My dear!'
If, by strange chance, a modest blush be raised,
Be sure my fine complexion must be praised.
My garments always must be new and gay,
And feasts still kept upon my wedding day.
Then must my nurse be pleased, and favourite maid:
And endless treats and endless visits paid
To a long train of kindred, friends, allies:
All this thou say'st, and all thou say'st are lies.

On Jenkin, too, you cast a squinting eye:

What! can your 'prentice raise your jealousy?
Fresh are his ruddy cheeks, his forehead fair,
And like the burnish'd gold his curling hair.
But clear thy wrinkled brow, and quit thy sorrow,
I'd scorn your 'prentice should you die to-morrow.

Why are thy chests all lock'd? on what design?
Are not thy worldly goods and treasures mine?
Sir, I'm no fool; nor shall you, by St John,
Have goods and body to yourself alone.
One you shall quit, in spite of both your eyes—
I heed not, I, the bolts, the locks, the spies.
If you had wit, you'd say, 'Go where you will,
Dear spouse! I credit not the tales they tell:
Take all the freedoms of a married life;
I know thee for a virtuous, faithful wife.'

Lord! when you have enough, what need you care
How merrily soever others fare?
Though all the day I give and take delight,
Doubt not, sufficient will be left at night.
'Tis but a just and rational desire
To light a taper at a neighbour's fire.
There's danger too, you think, in rich array,
And none can long be modest that are gay.
The cat, if you but singe her tabby skin,
The chimney keeps, and sits content within:
But once grown sleek, will from her corner run,
Sport with her tail, and wanton in the sun:
She licks her fair round face, and frisks abroad
To show her fur, and to be catterwaw'd.

Lo! thus, my friends, I wrought to my desires
These three right ancient venerable sires.
I told 'em, Thus you say, and thus you do;
And told 'em false, but Jenkin swore 'twas true.
I, like a dog, could bite as well as whine,
And first complain'd whene'er the guilt was mine.
I tax'd them oft with wenching and amours,
When their weak legs scarce dragg'd them out of doors
And swore, the rambles that I took by night
Were all to spy what damsels they bedight:
That colour brought me many hours of mirth;
For all this wit is given us from our birth.
Heaven gave to woman the peculiar grace
To spin, to weep, and cully human race.
By this nice conduct and this prudent course,
By murmuring, wheedling, stratagem, and force,

I still prevail'd, and would be in the right,
Or curtain lectures made a restless night.
If once my husband's arm was o'er my side,
'What! so familiar with your spouse?' I cried:
I levièd first a tax upon his need;
Then let him—'twas a nicety indeed!
Let all mankind this certain maxim hold;
Marry who will, our sex is to be sold.
With empty hands no tassels you can lure,
But fulsome love for gain we can endure;
For gold we love the impotent and old,
And heave, and pant, and kiss, and cling, for gold.
Yet with embraces curses oft I mix'd,
Then kiss'd again, and chid, and rail'd betwixt.
Well, I may make my will in peace, and die,
For not one word in man's arrears am I.
To drop a dear dispute I was unable,
E'en though the Pope himself had sat at table:
But when my point was gain'd, then thus I spoke:
'Billy, my dear, how sheepishly you look!
Approach, my spouse, and let me kiss thy cheek;
Thou shouldst be always thus, resign'd and meek!
Of Job's great patience since so oft you preach,
Well should you practise who so well can teach.
'Tis difficult to do, I must allow,
But I, my dearest! will instruct you how.
Great is the blessing of a prudent wife,
Who puts a period to domestic strife.
One of us two must rule, and one obey;
And since in man right reason bears the sway,
Let that frail thing, weak woman, have her way.
The wives of all my family have ruled
Their tender husbands, and their passions cool'd.
Fye! 'tis unmanly thus to sigh and groan:
What! would you have me to yourself alone?
Why, take me, love! take all and every part!
Here's your revenge! you love it at your heart.
Would I vouchsafe to sell what nature gave,
You little think what custom I could have.
But see! I'm all your own—nay, hold—for shame!
What means my dear?—indeed, you are to blame.'

Thus with my first three lords I pass'd my life,
A very woman, and a very wife.
What sums from these old spouses I could raise,
Procured young husbands in my riper days.
Though past my bloom, not yet decay'd was I,
Wanton and wild, and chatter'd like a pie.

In country-dances still I bore the bell,
And sung as sweet as evening Philomel.
To clear my quail-pipe, and refresh my soul,
Full oft I drain'd the spicy nut-brown bowl;
Rich luscious wines, that youthful blood improve,
And warm the swelling veins to feats of love:
For 'tis as sure as cold engenders hail,
A liquorish mouth must have a lecherous tail:
Wine lets no lover unrewarded go,
As all true gamesters by experience know.

But oh, good gods! whene'er a thought I cast
On all the joys of youth and beauty past,
To find in pleasures I have had my part,
Still warms me to the bottom of my heart.
This wicked world was once my dear delight;
Now, all my conquests, all my charms, good night!
The flour consumed, the best that now I can
Is e'en to make my market of the bran.

My fourth dear spouse was not exceeding true;
He kept, 'twas thought, a private miss or two:
But all that score I paid—As how? you'll say,
Not with my body, in a filthy way;
But I so dress'd, and danced, and drank, and dined,
And view'd a friend with eyes so very kind,
As stung his heart, and made his marrow fry,
With burning rage and frantic jealousy
His soul, I hope, enjoys eternal glory,
For here on earth I was his purgatory.
Oft, when his shoe the most severely wrung,
He put on careless airs, and sat and sung.
How sore I gall'd him only heaven could know,
And he that felt, and I that caused the woe:
He died, when last from pilgrimage I came,
With other gossips from Jerusalem,
And now lies buried underneath a rood,
Fair to be seen, and rear'd of honest wood:
A tomb, indeed, with fewer sculptures graced
Than that Mausolus' pious widow placed,
Or where enshrined the great Darius lay;
But cost on graves is merely thrown away.
The pit fill'd up, with turf we cover'd o'er;
So bless the good man's soul! I say no more.

Now for my fifth loved lord, the last and best;
(Kind heaven afford him everlasting rest!)
Full hearty was his love, and I can show

The tokens on my ribs in black and blue;
Yet with a knack my heart he could have won,
While yet the smart was shooting in the bone.
How quaint an appetite in woman reigns!
Free gifts we scorn, and love what costs us pains:
Let men avoid us, and on them we leap;
A glutted market makes provisions cheap.

In pure goodwill I took this jovial spark,
Of Oxford he, a most egregious clerk.
He boarded with a widow in the town,
A trusty gossip, one dame Alison;
Full well the secrets of my soul she knew,
Better than e'er our parish priest could do.
To her I told whatever could befall:
Had but my husband piss'd against a wall,
Or done a thing that might have cost his life,
She—and my niece—and one more worthy wife,
Had known it all: what most he would conceal,
To these I made no scruple to reveal.
Oft has he blush'd from ear to ear for shame
That e'er he told a secret to his dame.

It so befell, in holy time of Lent,
That oft a day I to this gossip went;
(My husband, thank my stars, was out of town)
From house to house we rambled up and down,
This clerk, myself, and my good neighbour, Alse,
To see, be seen, to tell, and gather tales.
Visits to every church we daily paid,
And march'd in every holy masquerade;
The stations duly, and the vigils kept;
Not much we fasted, but scarce ever slept.
At sermons, too, I shone in scarlet gay:
The wasting moth ne'er spoil'd my best array;
The cause was this, I wore it every day.

'Twas when fresh May her early blossoms yields,
This clerk and I were walking in the fields.
We grew so intimate, I can't tell how,
I pawn'd my honour, and engaged my vow,
If e'er I laid my husband in his urn,
That he, and only he, should serve my turn.
We straight struck hands, the bargain was agreed;
I still have shifts against a time of need:
The mouse that always trusts to one poor hole
Can never be a mouse of any soul.

I vow'd I scarce could sleep since first I knew him,
And durst be sworn he had bewitch'd me to him
If e'er I slept, I dream'd of him alone,
And dreams foretell, as learned men have shown:
All this I said; but dreams, sirs, I had none:
I follow'd but my crafty crony's lore,
Who bid me tell this lie—and twenty more.

Thus day by day, and month by mouth we pass'd;
It pleased the Lord to take my spouse at last.
I tore my gown, I soil'd my locks with dust,
And beat my breasts, as wretched widows must.
Before my face my handkerchief I spread,
To hide the flood of tears I did not shed.
The good man's coffin to the church was borne;
Around, the neighbours, and my clerk, too, mourn:
But as he march'd, good gods! he show'd a pair
Of legs and feet so clean, so strong, so fair!
Of twenty winters' age he seem'd to be;
I (to say truth) was twenty more than he;
But vigorous still, a lively buxom dame,
And had a wondrous gift to quench a flame.
A conjuror once, that deeply could divine,
Assured me Mars in Taurus was my sign.
As the stars order'd, such my life has been:
Alas, alas! that ever love was sin!
Fair Venus gave me fire and sprightly grace,
And Mars assurance and a dauntless face.
By virtue of this powerful constellation,
I follow'd always my own inclination.

But to my tale: A month scarce pass'd away,
With dance and song we kept the nuptial day.
All I possess'd I gave to his command,
My goods and chattels, money, house, and land;
But oft repented, and repent it still;
He proved a rebel to my sovereign will;
Nay, once, by heaven! he struck me on the face;
Hear but the fact, and judge yourselves the case.

Stubborn as any lioness was I,
And knew full well to raise my voice on high;
As true a rambler as I was before,
And would be so in spite of all he swore.
He against this right sagely would advise,
And old examples set before my eyes;
Tell how the Roman matrons led their life,
Of Gracchus' mother, and Duilius' wife;

And close the sermon, as beseem'd his wit,
With some grave sentence out of Holy Writ.
Oft would he say, 'Who builds his house on sands,
Pricks his blind horse across the fallow lands;
Or lets his wife abroad with pilgrims roam,
Deserves a fool's cap and long ears at home.'
All this avail'd not, for whoe'er he be
That tells my faults, I hate him mortally!
And so do numbers more, I'll boldly say,
Men, women, clergy, regular, and lay.

My spouse (who was, you know, to learning bred)
A certain treatise oft at evening read,
Where divers authors (whom the devil confound
For all their lies) were in one volume bound:
Valerius whole, and of St Jerome part;
Chrysippus and Tertullian, Ovid's Art,
Solomon's Proverbs, Eloisa's Loves,
And many more than, sure, the Church approves.
More legends were there here of wicked wives
Than good in all the Bible and saints' lives.
Who drew the lion vanquish'd? 'Twas a man:
But could we women write as scholars can,
Men should stand mark'd with far more wickedness
Than all the sons of Adam could redress.
Love seldom haunts the breast where learning lies,
And Venus sets ere Mercury can rise.
Those play the scholars who can't play the men,
And use that weapon which they have, their pen:
When old, and past the relish of delight,
Then down they sit, and in their dotage write,
That not one woman keeps her marriage-vow.
(This by the way, but to my purpose now:)

It chanced my husband, on a winter's night,
Read in this book aloud with strange delight,
How the first female (as the Scriptures show)
Brought her own spouse and all his race to woe;
How Samson fell; and he whom Dejanire
Wrapp'd in th' envenom'd shirt, and set on fire;
How cursed Eriphyle her lord betray'd,
And the dire ambush Clytemnestra laid;
But what most pleased him was the Cretan dame
And husband-bull—Oh, monstrous! fye, for shame!

He had by heart the whole detail of woe
Xantippe made her good man undergo;
How oft she scolded in a day he knew,

How many pisspots on the sage she threw;
Who took it patiently, and wiped his head:
'Rain follows thunder,' that was all he said.

He read how Arius to his friend complain'd
A fatal tree was growing in his land,
On which three wives successively had twined
A sliding noose, and waver'd in the wind.
'Where grows this plant,' replied the friend, 'oh! where?
For better fruit did never orchard bear:
Give me some slip of this most blissful tree,
And in my garden planted it shall be!'

Then how two wives their lords' destruction prove,
Through hatred one, and one through too much love;
That for her husband mix'd a poisonous draught,
And this for lust an amorous philtre bought:
The nimble juice soon seized his giddy head,
Frantic at night, and in the morning dead.

How some with swords their sleeping lords have slain,
And some have hammer'd nails into their brain,
And some have drench'd them with a deadly potion:
All this he read, and read with great devotion.

Long time I heard, and swell'd, and blush'd, and frown'd;
But when no end of these vile tales I found,
When still he read, and laugh'd, and read again,
And half the night was thus consumed in vain,
Provoked to vengeance, three large leaves I tore,
And with one buffet fell'd him on the floor.
With that my husband in a fury rose,
And down he settled me with hearty blows.
I groan'd, and lay extended on my side;
'Oh! thou hast slain me for my wealth!' I cried,
'Yet I forgive thee—take my last embrace—'
He wept, kind soul! and stoop'd to kiss my face:
I took him such a box as turn'd him blue,
Then sigh'd, and cried, 'Adieu, my dear, adieu!'

But after many a hearty struggle past,
I condescended to be pleased at last.
Soon as he said, 'My mistress and my wife!
Do what you list the term of all your life,'
I took to heart the merits of the cause,
And stood content to rule by wholesome laws;
Received the reins of absolute command,
With all the government of house and land,

And empire o'er his tongue and o'er his hand.
As for the volume that reviled the dames,
'Twas torn to fragments, and condemn'd to flames.

Now, Heaven, on all my husbands gone bestow
Pleasures above for tortures felt below:
That rest they wish'd for, grant them in the grave,
And bless those souls my conduct help'd to save!

Alexander Pope – A Short Biography

Alexander Pope was born in Lombard Street, London, on the 21st of May 1688—the year of the Revolution. His father was a linen-merchant, in thriving circumstances, and said to have noble blood in his veins. His mother was Edith or Editha Turner, daughter of William Turner, Esq., of York. Mr Carruthers, in his excellent Life of the Poet, mentions that there was an Alexander Pope, a clergyman, in the remote parish of Reay, in Caithness, who rode all the way to Twickenham to pay his great namesake a visit, and was presented by him with a copy of the subscription edition of the "Odyssey," in five volumes quarto, which is still preserved by his descendants. Pope's father had made about £10,000 by trade; but being a Roman Catholic, and fond of a country life, he retired from business shortly after the Revolution, at the early age of forty-six. He resided first at Kensington, and then in Binfield, in the neighbourhood of Windsor Forest. He is said to have put his money in a strong box, and to have lived on the principal. His great delight was in his garden; and both he and his wife seem to have cherished the warmest interest in their son, who was very delicate in health, and their only child. Pope's study is still preserved in Binfield; and on the lawn, a cypress-tree which he is said to have planted, is pointed out.

Pope was a premature and precocious child. His figure was deformed—his back humped—his stature short (four feet six inches)—his legs and arms disproportionably long. He was sometimes compared to a spider, and sometimes to a windmill. The only mark of genius lay in his bright and piercing eye. He was sickly in constitution, and required and received great tenderness and care. Once, when three years old, he narrowly escaped from an angry cow, but was wounded in the throat. He was remarkable as a child for his amiable temper; and from the sweetness of his voice, received the name of the Little Nightingale. His aunt gave him his first lessons in reading, and he soon became an enthusiastic lover of books; and by copying printed characters, taught himself to write. When eight years old, he was placed under the care of the family priest, one Bannister, who taught him the Latin and Greek grammars together. He was next removed to a Catholic seminary at Twyford, near Winchester; and while there, read Ogilby's "Homer" and Sandys's "Ovid" with great delight. He had not been long at this school till he wrote a severe lampoon, of two hundred lines' length, on his master—so truly was the "boy the father of the man"—for which demi-Dunciad he was severely flogged. His father, offended at this, removed him to a London school, kept by a Mr Deane. This man taught the poet nothing; but his residence in London gave him the opportunity of attending the theatres. With these he was so captivated, that he wrote a kind of play, which was acted by his schoolfellows, consisting of speeches from Ogilby's "Iliad," tacked together with verses of his own. He became acquainted with Dryden's works, and went to Wills's coffee-house to see him. He says, "Virgilium tantum vidi." Such transient meetings of literary orbs are among the most interesting passages in biography. Thus met Galileo with Milton, Milton with Dryden, Dryden with Pope, and Burns with Scott. Carruthers strikingly remarks, "Considering the perils and uncertainties of a literary life—its precarious rewards, feverish anxieties, mortifications, and disappointments, joined to the tyranny of the Tonsons and Lintots, and the malice and envy of dunces, all of which Dryden had long and bitterly experienced—the aged poet could hardly have looked at the delicate and deformed boy, whose preternatural acuteness and sensibility were seen in his dark eyes, without a feeling approaching to grief, had he known that he was to fight a battle like that under which he was himself then sinking, even though the Temple of Fame should at length open to receive him." At twelve, he wrote the "Ode to Solitude;" and shortly after, his satirical piece on Elkanah Settle, and some of his translations and imitations. His next period, he says, was in Windsor Forest, where for several years he did nothing but read the classics and indite poetry. He wrote a tragedy, a comedy, and four books of an Epic called "Alexander," all of which afterwards he committed to the flames. He translated also a portion of Statius, and Cicero "De Senectute," and "thought himself the greatest genius that ever was." His father encouraged him in his studies, and when his verses did not please him, sent him back to "new turn" them, saying, "These are not good rhymes." His principal favourites were Virgil's "Eclogues," in Latin; and in English, Spencer, Waller, and Dryden—admiring Spencer, we presume, for his luxuriant fancy, Waller for his smooth versification, and Dryden for his vigorous sense and vivid sarcasm. In the Forest, he became acquainted with Sir William Trumbull, the retired secretary of state, a man of general accomplishments, who read, rode, conversed with the youthful poet; introduced him to old Wycherley, the dramatist; and was of material service to his views. With Wycherley, who was old, doted, and excessively vain, Pope did not continue long intimate. A coldness, springing from some criticisms which the youth ventured to make on the veteran's poetry, crept in between them. Walsh of Abberley, in Worcestershire, a man of good sense and taste, became, after a perusal of the "Pastorals" in MS., a warm friend and kind adviser of Pope's, who has immortalised him in more than one of his poems. Walsh told Pope that there had never hitherto appeared in Britain a poet who was at once great and correct, and exhorted him to aim at accuracy and elegance.

When fifteen, he visited London, in order to acquire a more thorough knowledge of French and Italian. At sixteen, he wrote the "Pastorals," and a portion of "Windsor Forest," although they were not published for some time afterwards. By his incessant exertions, he now began to feel his constitution injured. He imagined himself dying, and sent farewell letters to all his friends, including the Abbé Southcot. This gentleman communicated Pope's case to Dr Ratcliffe, who gave him some medical directions; by following which, the poet recovered. He was advised to relax in his studies, and to ride daily; and he prudently followed the advice. Many years afterwards, he repaid the benevolent Abbé by procuring for him, through Sir Robert Walpole, the nomination to an abbey in Avignon. This is only one of many proofs that, notwithstanding his waspish temper, and his no small share of malice as well as vanity, there was a warm heart in our poet.

In 1707, Pope became acquainted with Michael Blount of Maple, Durham, near Reading; whose two sisters, Martha and Teresa, he has commemorated in various verses. On his connexion with these ladies, some mystery rests. Bowles has strongly and plausibly urged that it was not of the purest or most creditable order. Others have contended that it did not go further than the manners of the age sanctioned; and they say, "a much greater license in conversation and in epistolary correspondence was permitted between the sexes than in our decorous age!" We are not careful to try and settle such a delicate question—only we are inclined to suspect, that when common decency quits the words of male and female parties in their mutual communications, it is a very ample charity that can suppose it to adhere to their actions. And nowhere do we find grosser language than in some of Pope's prose epistles to the Blounts.

His "Pastorals," after having been handed about in MS., and shewn to such reputed judges as Lord Halifax, Lord Somers, Garth, Congreve, &c., were at last, in 1709, printed in the sixth volume of Tonson's

"Miscellanies." Like all well-finished commonplaces, they were received with instant and universal applause. It is humiliating to contrast the reception of these empty echoes of inspiration, these agreeable centos, with that of such genuine, although faulty poems, as Keat's "Endymion," Shelley's "Queen Mab," and Wordsworth's "Lyrical Ballads." Two years later, (in 1711), a far better and more characteristic production from his pen was ushered anonymously into the world. This was the "Essay on Criticism," a work which he had first written in prose, and which discovers a ripeness of judgment, a clearness of thought, a condensation of style, and a command over the information he possesses, worthy of any age in life, and almost of any mind in time. It serves, indeed, to shew what Pope's true forte was. That lay not so much in poetry, as in the knowledge of its principles and laws, not so much in creation, as in criticism. He was no Homer or Shakspeare; but he might have been nearly as acute a judge of poetry as Aristotle, and nearly as eloquent an expounder of the rules of art and the glories of genius as Longinus.

In the same year, Pope printed "The Rape of the Lock," in a volume of Miscellanies. Lord Petre had, much in the way described by the poet, stolen a lock of Miss Belle Fermor's hair, a feat which led to an estrangement between the families. Pope set himself to reconcile them by this beautiful poem, a poem which has embalmed at once the quarrel and the reconciliation to all future time. In its first version, the machinery was awanting, the "lock" was a desert, the "rape" a natural event, the small infantry of sylphs and gnomes were slumbering uncreated in the poet's mind; but in the next edition he contrived to introduce them in a manner so easy and so exquisite, as to remind you of the variations which occur in dreams, where one wonder seems softly to slide into the bosom of another, and where beautiful and fantastic fancies grow suddenly out of realities, like the bud from the bough, or the fairy-seeming wing of the summer-cloud from the stern azure of the heavens.

A little after this, Pope became acquainted with a far greater, better, and truer man than himself, Joseph Addison. Warburton, and others, have sadly misrepresented the connexion between these two famous wits, as well as their relative intellectual positions. Addison was a more amiable and childlike person than Pope. He had much more, too, of the Christian. He was not so elaborately polished and furbished as the author of "The Rape of the Lock;" but he had, naturally, a finer and richer genius. Pope found early occasion for imagining Addison his disguised enemy. He gave him a hint of his intention to introduce the machinery into "The Rape of the Lock." Of this, Addison disapproved, and said it was a delicious little thing already—merum sal. This, Pope, and some of his friends, have attributed to jealousy; but it is obvious that Addison could not foresee the success with which the machinery was to be managed, and did foresee the difficulties connected with tinkering such an exquisite production. We may allude here to the circumstances which, at a later date, produced an estrangement between these celebrated men. When Tickell, Addison's friend, published the first book of the "Iliad," in opposition to Pope's version, Addison gave it the preference. This moved Pope's indignation, and led him to assert that it was Addison's own composition. In this conjecture he was supported by Edward Young, who had known Tickell long and intimately, and had never heard of him having written at college, as was averred, this translation. It is now, however, we believe, certain, from the MS. which still exists, that Tickell was the real author. A coldness, from this date, began between Pope and Addison. An attempt to reconcile them only made matters worse; and at last the breach was rendered irremediable by Pope's writing the famous character of his rival, afterwards inserted in the Prologue to the Satires, a portrait drawn with the perfection of polished malice and bitter sarcasm, but which seems more a caricature than a likeness. Whatever Addison's faults, his conduct to Pope did not deserve such a return. The whole passage is only one of those painful incidents which disgrace the history of letters, and prove how much spleen, ingratitude, and baseness often co-exist with the highest parts. The words of Pope are as true now as ever they were—"the life of a wit is a warfare upon earth;" and a warfare in which poisoned missiles and every variety of falsehood are still common. We may also here mention, that while the friendship of Pope and Addison lasted, the former contributed the well-known prologue to the latter's "Cato."

One of Pope's most intimate friends in his early days was Henry Cromwell—a distant relative of the great Oliver—a gentleman of fortune, gallantry, and literary taste, who became his agreeable and fascinating, but somewhat dangerous, companion. He is supposed to have initiated Pope into some of the fashionable follies of the town. At this time, Pope's popularity roused one of his most formidable foes against him. This was that Cobbett of criticism, old John Dennis, a man of strong natural powers, much learning, and a rich, coarse vein of humour; but irascible, vindictive, vain, and capricious. Pope had provoked him by an attack in his "Essay on Criticism," and the savage old man revenged himself by a running fire of fierce diatribes against that "Essay" and "The Rape of the Lock." Pope waited till Dennis had committed himself by a powerful but furious assault on Addison's "Cato" (most of which Johnson has preserved in his Life of Pope); and then, partly to court Addison, and partly to indulge his spleen at the critic, wrote a prose satire, entitled, "The Narrative of Dr Robert Norris on the Frenzy of J.D." In this, however, he overshot the mark; and Addison signified to him that he was displeased with the spirit of his narrative, an intimation which Pope keenly resented. This scornful dog would not eat the dirty pudding that was graciously flung to him; and Pope found that, without having conciliated Addison, he had made Dennis's furnace of hate against himself seven times hotter than before.

In 1712 appeared "The Messiah," "The Dying Christian to his Soul," "The Temple of Fame," and the "Elegy on the Memory of an Unfortunate Lady." Her story is still involved in mystery. Her name is said to have been Wainsbury. She was attached to a lover above her degree, some say to the Duke of Berry, whom she had met in her early youth in France. In despair of obtaining her desire, she hanged herself. It is curious, if true, that she was as deformed in person as Pope himself. Her family seems to have been noble. In 1713, he published "Windsor Forest," an "Ode on St Cecilia's Day," and several papers in the Guardian—one of them being an exquisitely ironical paper, comparing Phillip's pastorals with his own, and affecting to give them the preference—the extracts being so selected as to damage his rival's claims. This year, also, he wrote, although he did not publish, his fine epistle to Jervas, the painter. Pope was passionately fond of the art of painting, and practised it a good deal under Jervas's instructions, although he did not reach great proficiency. The prodigy has yet to be born who combines the characters of a great painter and a great poet.

About this time, Pope commenced preparations for the great work of translating Homer; and subscription-papers, accordingly, were issued. Dean Swift was now in England, and took a deep interest in the success of this undertaking, recommending it in coffee-houses, and introducing the subject and Pope's name to the leading Tories. Pope met the Dean for the first time in Berkshire, where, in one of his fits of savage disgust at the conflicting parties of the period, he had retired to the house of a clergyman, and an intimacy commenced which was only terminated by death. We have often regretted that Pope had not selected some author more suitable to his genius than Homer. Horace or Lucretius, or even Ovid, would have been more congenial. His imitations of Horace shew us what he might have made of a complete translation. What a brilliant thing a version of Lucretius, in the style of the "Essay on Man," would have been! And his "Rape of the Lock" proves that he had considerable sympathy with the elaborate fancy, although not with the meretricious graces of Ovid. But with Homer, the severely grand, the simple, the warlike, the lover and painter of all Nature's old original forms—the ocean, the mountains, and the stars—what thorough sympathy could a man have who never saw a real mountain or a battle, and whose enthusiasm for scenery was confined to purling brooks, trim gardens, artificial grottos, and the shades of Windsor Forest? Accordingly, his Homer, although a beautiful and sparkling poem, is not a satisfactory translation of the "Iliad," and still less of the "Odyssey." He has trailed along the naked lances of the Homeric lines so many flowers and leaves that you can hardly recognise them, and feel that their point is deadened and their power gone. This at least is our opinion; although many to this day continue to admire these translations, and have even said that if they are not Homer, they are something better.

The "Iliad" took him six years, and was a work which cost him much anxiety as well as labour, the more as his scholarship was far from profound. He was assisted in the undertaking by Parnell (who wrote the Life of Homer), by Broome, Jortin, and others. The first volume appeared in June 1715, and the other volumes followed at irregular intervals. He began it in 1712, his twenty-fifth year, and finished it in 1718, his thirtieth year. Previous to its appearance, his remuneration for his poems had been small, and his circumstances were embarrassed; but the result of the subscription, which amounted to £5320, 4s., rendered him independent for life.

While at Binfield, he had often visited London; and there, in the society of Howe, Garth, Parnell, and the rest, used to indulge in occasional excesses, which did his feeble constitution no good; and once, according to Colley Cibber, he narrowly escaped a serious scrape in a house of a certain description, Colley, by his own account, "helping out the tomtit for the sake of Homer!" This statement, indeed, Pope has denied; but his veracity was by no means his strongest point. After writing a "Farewell to London," he retired, in 1715, to Twickenham, along with his parents; and remained there, cultivating his garden, digging his grottos, and diversifying his walks, till the end of his days.

Some years before, he had become acquainted with Lady Mary Wortley Montague, the most brilliant woman of her age—witty, fascinating, beautiful, and accomplished—full of enterprise and spirit, too, although decidedly French in her tastes, manners, and character. Pope fell violently in love with her, and had her undoubtedly in his eye when writing "Eloisa and Abelard," which he did at Oxford in 1716, shortly after her going abroad, and which appeared the next year. His passion was not requited, nay, was treated with contempt and ridicule; and he became in after years a bitter enemy and foul-mouthed detractor of the lady, although after her return, in 1718, she resided near him at Twickenham, and they seemed outwardly on good terms.

In 1717, and the succeeding year, Pope lost successively his father, Parnell, Garth, and Rowe, and bitterly felt their loss. He finished, as we have seen, the "Iliad" in 1718; but the fifth and sixth volumes, which were the last, did not appear till 1720. Its success, which at the time was triumphant, roused against him the whole host of envy and detraction. Dennis, and all Grub Street with him, were moved to assail him. Pamphlets after pamphlets were published, all of which, after reading with writhing anguish, Pope had the resolution to bind up into volumes—a great collection of calumny, which he preserved, probably, for purposes of future revenge. His own friends, on the other hand, hailed his work with applause, Gay writing a most graceful and elegant poem, in ottava rima, entitled, "Mr Pope's Welcome Home from Greece," in which his different friends are pictured as receiving him home on the shores of Britain, after an absence of six years. Bentley, that stern old Grecian, avoided the extremes of a howling Grub Street on the one hand, and a flattering aristocracy on the other, and expressed what is, we think, the just opinion when he said, "It is a pretty poem, but it is not Homer."

In 1721, he issued a selection from the poems of Parnell, and prefixed a very beautiful dedication to the Earl of Oxford, commencing with—

"Such were the notes thy once-loved poet sung,
Till death untimely stopp'd his tuneful tongue.

Oh, just beheld and lost, admired and mourn'd,
With softest manners, gentlest arts adorn'd!"

In 1722, he engaged to translate the "Odyssey." He employed Broome and Fenton as his assistants in the work; and the portions translated by them were thought as good as his. He remunerated them very handsomely. Of this work, the first three quarto volumes appeared in 1725; and the fourth and fifth, which completed the work, the following year. Pope sold the copyright to Lintot for £600.

He was busy at this time, too, with an edition of Shakspeare, not quite worthy of either poet. It appeared in six volumes, quarto, in 1725. His preface was good, but he was deficient in antiquarian lore; and his mortification was extreme when Theobald, destined to figure in "The Dunciad," a mere plodding hack, not only in his "Shakspeare Restored," exposed many blunders in Pope's edition; but issued, some years afterwards, an edition of his own, which was much better received by the public.

In 1726, there was a great gathering of the Tory wits at Twickenham. Swift had come from Ireland, and resided for some time with Pope. Bolingbroke came over occasionally from Dawley; and Gay was often there to laugh with, and be laughed at by, the rest. Swift had "Gulliver's Travels"—the most ingenious and elaborate libel against man and God ever written—in his pocket, nearly ready for publication; and we may conceive the grim, sardonic smile with which he read it to his friends, and their tumultuous mirth. Gay was projecting his "Beggars' Opera," and Pope preparing some of his witty "Miscellanies." At the end of two months, the Dean was hurried home by the tidings of Stella's illness. He left the "Travels" behind him, for the copyright of which Pope procured £300, a sum counted then very large, and which Swift generously handed over to Pope.

In September this year, when returning in Lord Bolingbroke's coach from Dawley, the poet was overturned in a little rivulet near Twickenhan, and nearly drowned. The unfortunate little man! One is reminded of Gulliver's accident in the Brobdignagian cream-pot. In trying to break the glasses of the coach, which were down, he severely cut his right hand, and lost the use of two of his fingers, an addition to his other deformities not very desirable; and we suspect that Pope thought Voltaire (who had met him at Bolingbroke's) but a miserable comforter, when, in a letter of pretended condolence, he asked—"Is it possible that those fingers which have written 'The Rape of the Lock,' and dressed Homer so becomingly in an English coat, should have been so barbarously treated? Let the hand of Dennis or of your poetasters be cut off; yours is sacred." It was perhaps in keeping that those mutilated fingers were soon to be employed in attacking Dennis, and that the embittered poet was about, with the half of his hand, but with the whole of his heart, to write "The Dunciad."

In the end of April 1727, we find Swift again in Twickenham, where his irritation at the continued ascendancy of Sir Robert Walpole served to infuse more venom into the "Miscellanies" concocted between him and Pope, two volumes of which appeared in June this year. Gay, also, and the ingenious and admirable Dr Arbuthnot, contributed their quota to these volumes. Swift speedily fell ill with that giddiness and deafness which were the avant-couriers of his final malady; and in August he left Twickenham, and in October, London and England, for ever.

In these "Miscellanies" there appeared the famous "Memoirs of Martinus Scriblerus," written chiefly by Pope, in which he lashed the various proficients in the bathos, under the names of flying fishes, swallows, parrots, frogs, eels, &c., and appended the initials of well-known authors to each head. This roused Grub Street, whose malice had nearly fallen asleep, into fresh fury, and he was bitterly assailed in every possible form. Like Hyder Ali, he now—to travesty Burke—"in the recesses of a mind capacious of such things, determined to leave all Duncedom an everlasting monument of vengeance, and became at length so confident of his force, so collected in his might, that he made no secret whatever of his dreadful resolution, but, compounding all the materials of fun, sarcasm, irony, and invective, into one black cloud, he hung for a while on the declivities of Richmond Hill; and whilst the authors were idly and stupidly gazing on this menacing meteor which blackened all their horizon, it suddenly burst and poured down the whole of its contents on the garrets of Grub Street. Then issued a scene of (ludicrous) woe, the like of which no eye had seen, no heart conceived, and which no tongue can adequately tell. All the horrors of literary war before known or heard of—(MacFlecknoe, the Rehearsal, &c.)—were mercy to the new tempest of havoc which burst from the brain of this remorseless poet. A storm of universal laughter filled every bookseller's shop, and penetrated into the remotest attics. The miserable dunces, in part, were stricken mad with rage—in part, dumb with consternation. Some fled for refuge to ale, and others to ink; while not a few fell, or feared to fall, into the 'jaws of famine.'" This singular poem was written in 1727. It was first printed surreptitiously (i.e., with the connivance of the author) in Dublin, and then reprinted in London. The first perfect edition, however, did not appear in London till 1729. On the day of its publication, according to Pope, a crowd of authors besieged the publisher's shop; and by entreaties, threats, nay, cries of treason, tried to hinder its appearance. What a scene it must have been—of teeth gnashing above ragged coats, and eyes glaring through old periwigs—of faces livid with famine and ferocity; while, to complete the confusion, hawkers, booksellers, and even lords, were mixed with the crowd, clamouring for its issue! And as, says Pope, "there is no stopping a torrent with a finger, out it came." The consequence he had foreseen. A universal howl of rage and pain burst from the aggrieved dunces, on whose naked sides the hot pitch had fallen. They pushed their rejoinders beyond the limits of civilised literary warfare; and although Pope had been coarse in his language, they were coarser far, and their blackguardism was not redeemed by wit or genius. Pope felt, or seemed to feel, entire indifference as to these assaults. On some of them, indeed, he could afford to look down with contempt, on account of their obvious animus and gross language. Others, again, were neutralised by the fact, that their authors had provoked reprisals by their previous insults or ingratitude to Pope. Many, however, were too obscure for his notice; and some, such as Aaron Hill and Bentley, did not deserve to be classed with the Theobalds and Ralphs. To Hill, he, after some finessing, was compelled to make an apology. Altogether, although this production increased Pope's fame, and the conception of his power, it did not tend to shew him in the most amiable light, or perhaps to promote his own comfort or peace of mind. After having emptied out his bile in "The Dunciad," he ought to have become mellower in temper, and resigned satire for ever. He continued, on the contrary, as ill-natured as before; and although he afterwards flew at higher game, the iron had entered into his soul, and he remained a satirist, and therefore an unhappy man, for life.

In 1731 appeared an "Epistle on Taste," which was very favourably received; only his enemies accused him of having satirised the Duke of Chandos in it, a man who had befriended Pope, and had lent him money. Pope denied the charge, although it is very possible, both from his own temperament, and from the frequent occurrence of similar cases of baseness in literary life, that it may have been true. Nothing is more common than for those who have been most liberally helped, to become first the secret, and then the open, enemies of their benefactors. In 1732 appeared his epistle on "The Use of Riches," addressed to Lord Bathurst. These two epistles were afterwards incorporated in his "Moral Essays."

As far back as 1725, Pope had been revolving the subject of the "Essay on Man;" and, indeed, some of its couplets remind you of "pebbles which had long been rolled over and polished in the ocean of his mind." It has been asserted, but not proved, that Lord Bolingbroke gave him the outline of this essay in prose. It is unquestionable, indeed, that Bolingbroke exercised influence over Pope's mind, and may have suggested some of the thoughts in the Essay; but it is not probable that a man like Pope would have set himself on such a subject simply to translate from another's mind. He published the first epistle of the Essay, in 1732, anonymously, as an experiment, and had the satisfaction to see it successful. It was received with rapture, and passed through several editions ere the author was known; although we must say that the value of this reception is considerably lessened, when we remember that the critics could not have been very acute who did not detect Pope's "fine Roman hand" in every sentence of this brilliant but most unsatisfactory and shallow performance.

In the same year died dear, simple-minded Gay, who found in Pope a sincere mourner, and an elegant elegiast; and on the 7th of June 1733, expired good old Mrs Pope, at the age of ninety-four. Pope, who had always been a dutiful son, erected an obelisk in his own grounds to her memory, with a simple but striking inscription in Latin. During this year, he published the third part of the "Essay on Man," an epistle to Lord Cobham, On the Knowledge and Characters of Man, and an Imitation of the First Satire of the Second Book of Horace. In this last, he attacks, in the most brutal style, his former love Lady Mary W. Montague, who replied in a piece of coarse cleverness, entitled, "Verses to the Imitator of the First Satire of the Second Book of Horace,"—verses in which she was assisted by Lord Harvey, another of Pope's victims. He wrote, but was prudent enough to suppress, an ironical reply.

In 1734 appeared his very clever and highly-finished epistle to Dr Arbuthnot (now entitled the "Prologue to the Satires"), who was then languishing toward death. Arbuthnot, from his deathbed, solemnly advised Pope to regulate his satire, and seems to have been afraid of his personal safety from his numerous foes. Pope replied in a manly but self-defensive style. He is said about this time to have in his walks carried arms, and had a large dog as his protector; but none of the duncos had courage enough to assail him. Dennis, who was no dunce, might have ventured on it—but he had become miserably infirm, poor, and blind; and Pope had heaped coals of fire on his head, by contributing a Prologue to a play which was acted for his behoof.

Our author's life becomes now little else than a record of multiplying labours and increasing infirmities. In 1734 appeared the fourth part of the "Essay on Man," and the Second Satire of the Second Book of Horace. In 1735 were issued his "Characters of Women: An Epistle to a Lady" (Martha Blount). In this appears his famous character of Atossa—the Duchess of Marlborough. It is said—we fear too truly—that these lines being shewn to her Grace, as a character of the Duchess of Buckingham, she recognised in them her own likeness, and bribed Pope with a thousand pounds to suppress it. He did so religiously—as long as she was alive—and then published it! In the same year he printed a second volume of his "Miscellaneous Works," in folio and quarto, uniform with the "Iliad" and "Odyssey," including a versification of the Satires of Donne; also, anonymously, a production disgraceful to his memory, entitled, "Sober Advice from Horace to the Young Gentlemen about Town," in which he commits many gross indecorums of language, and annexes the name of the great Bentley to several indecent notes. It is said that Bentley, when he read the pamphlet, cried, "'Tis an impudent dog, but I talked against his Homer, and the portentous cub never forgives."

The "Essay on Man" and the "Moral Epistles" were designed to be parts of a great system of ethics, which Pope had long revolved in his mind, and wished to incarnate in poetry. At this time occurred the strange, mysterious circumstances connected with the publication of his letters. It seems that, in 1729, Pope had recalled from his correspondents the letters he had written them, of many of which he had kept no copies. He was induced to this by the fact, that after Henry Cromwell's death, his mistress, Mrs Thomas, who was in indigent circumstances, had sold the letters which had passed between Pope and her keeper, to Curll the bookseller, who had published them without scruple. When Pope obtained his correspondence, he, according to his own statement, burned a great many and laid past the others, after having had a copy of them taken, and deposited in Lord Oxford's library. And his charge against Curll was, that he obtained surreptitiously some of these letters, and published them without Pope's consent. But, ere we come to the circumstances of the publication, several other things require to be noticed. In 1733, Curll, anxious to publish a Life of Pope, advertised for information; and, in consequence, one P.T., who professed to be an old friend of Pope's and his father's, wrote Curll a letter, giving an account of Pope's ancestry, which tallied exactly with what Pope himself, in a note to one of his poems, furnished the following year. P.T., in a second letter, offered to the publisher a large collection of Pope's letters, and inclosed a copy of an advertisement he had drawn out to be published by Curll. Strange as it seems, Curll took no notice of the proposal till 1735, when, having accidentally turned up a copy of P.T.'s advertisement, he sent it to Pope, with a letter requesting an interview, and mentioning that he had some papers of P.T.'s in reference to his family history, which he would shew him. Pope replied by three advertisements in the papers, denying all knowledge of P.T. or his collection of letters or MSS. P.T. then wrote Curll that he had printed the letters at his own expense, seeking a sum of money for them, and appointing an interview at a tavern to shew him the sheets. This was countermanded the next day, P.T. professing to be afraid of Pope and his "bravoes," although how Pope was to know of this meeting was, according to Curll, "the cream of the jest."

Soon after, a round, fat man, with a clergyman's gown and a barrister's band, called on Curll, at ten o'clock at night. He said his name was Smith, that he was a cousin of P.T.'s, and shewed the book in sheets, along with about a dozen of the original letters. After a good deal of negotiation with this personage, Curll obtained fifty copies of P.T.'s printed copies, and issued a flaming advertisement announcing the publication of Pope's letters for thirty years, and stating that the original MSS. were lying at his shop, and might be seen by any who chose, although not a single MS. seems to have been delivered. Smith, the day that the advertisement appeared, handed over, for a sum of money, about three hundred volumes to Curll. But as in the advertisement it was stated that various letters of lords were included, and as there is a law amongst regulations of the Upper House that no peer's letters can be published without his consent, at the instance of the Earl of Jersey, and in consequence, too, of an advertisement of Pope's, the books were seized, and Curll, and the printer of the paper where the advertisement appeared, were ordered to appear at the bar for breach of privilege. P.T. wrote Curll to tell him to conceal all that passed between him and the publisher, and promising him more valuable letters still. Curll, however, told the whole story; and as, when the books were examined, not a single lord's letter was found among them, Curll was acquitted, his books restored to him, the lords saying that they had been made the tools of Pope; and he proceeded to advertise the correspondence, in terms most insulting to Pope, who now felt himself compelled (!) to print, by subscription, his genuine letters, which, when printed, turned out, strange to tell, to be identical with those published by the rapacious bookseller! On viewing the whole transaction, we incline with Johnson, Warton, Bowles, Macaulay, and Carruthers, to look upon it as one of Pope's ape-like stratagems—to believe that P.T. was himself, Smith his agent, and that his objects were partly to outwit Curll, to mystify the public, to gratify that strange love of manoeuvring which dwelt as strongly in him as in any match-making mamma, and to attract interest and attention to the genuine correspondence when it should appear. Pope, it was said, could not "drink tea without a stratagem," and far less publish his correspondence without a series of contemptible tricks—tricks, however, in which he was true to his nature—that being a curious compound of the woman and the wit, the monkey and the genius.

In 1737, four of his Imitations of Horace were published, and in the next year appeared two Dialogues, each entitled "1738," which now form the Epilogue to the Satires. One of them was issued on the same day with Johnson's "London." In that year, too, he published his "Universal Prayer,"—a singular specimen of latitudinarian thought, expressed in a loose simplicity of language, quite unusual with its author. The next year he had intended to signalise by a third Dialogue, which he commenced in a vigorous style, but which he did not finish, owing to the dread of a prosecution before the Lords; and with the exception of letters (one of them interesting, as his last to Swift), his pen was altogether idle. In 1740, he did nothing but edit an edition of select Italian Poets. This year, Crousaz, a Swiss professor of note, having attacked (we think most justly) the "Essay on Man" as a mere Pagan prolusion—a thin philosophical smile cast on the Gordian knot of the mystery of the universe, instead of a sword cutting, or trying to cut, it in sunder—Warburton, a man of much talent and learning, but of more astuteness and anxiety to exalt himself, came forward to the rescue, and, with a mixture of casuistical cunning and real ingenuity, tried, as some one has it, "to make Pope a Christian," although, even in Warburton's hands, like the dying Donald Bane in "Waverley," he "makes but a queer Christian after all;" and his system, essentially Pantheistic, contrives to ignore the grand Scripture principles of a Fall, of a Divine Redeemer, of a Future World, and the glorious light or darkness which these and other Christian doctrines cast upon the Mystery of Man. If, however, Warburton, with all his scholastic subtlety, failed to make Pope a Christian, he made him a warm friend; Allen, Pope's acquaintance, a rich father-in-law; and himself, by and by, the Bishop of Gloucester. Sophistry has seldom, although sometimes, been thus richly rewarded.

The last scene of Pope's tiny and tortured existence was now at hand. But ere it closed, it must close like Dryden's, characteristically, with an author's quarrel. Colley Cibber had long been a favourite of Pope's ire, and had as often retorted scorn, till at last, by laughing upon the stage at Pope's play (partly Gay's), entitled, "Three Hours After Marriage," he roused the bard almost to frenzy; and Pope set to work to remodel "The Dunciad;" and, dethroning Theobald, set up Cibber as the lawful King of the Dull, a most unfortunate substitution, since, while Theobald was the ideal of stolid, solemn stupidity, Cibber was gay, light, pert, and clever; full of pluck, too, and who overflowed in reply, with pamphlets which gave Pope both a headache and a heartache whenever he perused them.

Pope had never been strong, and for many years the variety and multitude of his frailties had been increasing. He had habitually all his life been tormented with headaches, for which he found the steam of strong coffee the chief remedy. He had hurt his stomach, too, by indulging in excess of stimulating viands, such as potted lampreys, and in copious and frequent drams. He was assailed at last by dropsy and asthma; and on the 30th of May 1744, he breathed his last, fifty-six years of age. He had long, he said, "been tired of the world," and died with philosophic composure and serenity. He took the sacrament according to the form of the Roman Catholic Church; but merely, he said, because it "looked right." A little before his death, he called for his desk, and began an essay on the immortality of the soul, and on those material things which tend to weaken or to strengthen it for immortality, enumerating generous wines as among the latter influences, and spirituous liquors among the former! His last words were, "There is nothing that is meritorious but virtue and friendship; and, indeed, friendship itself is only a part of virtue." Thus, "motionless and moanless," without a word about Christ—the slightest syllable of repentance—and with a scrap of heathen morality in his mouth, died the brilliant Alexander Pope. Who is ready to say, "May my last end be like his"? His favourite Martha Blount behaved, according to some accounts, with disgusting unconcern on the occasion. So true it is, "there is no friendship among the wicked," even although the heartless Bolingbroke, too, was by, and seems to have succeeded in squeezing out some crocodile tears, as he bent over the dying poet, and said, "O God! what is man?" His remains were, according to his wish, deposited in Twickenham church, near his parents, where the single letter P on the stone alone distinguishes the spot.

Pope's character, apart from his poetry, which we intend criticising in our next volume, was not specially interesting or elevated. He was a spoiled child, a small self-tormentor, full to bursting with petty spites, mean animosities, and unfounded jealousies. While he sought, with the fury of a pampered slave, to trample on those authors that were beneath him in rank or in popularity, he could on all occasions fawn with the sycophancy of a eunuch upon the noble, the rich, and the powerful. Hazlitt speaks of Moore as a "pug-dog barking from the lap of a lady of quality at inferior passengers." The description is far more applicable to Pope. We have much allowance to make for the influence exerted on his mind by his singularly crooked frame and sickly habit of body, by his position as belonging to a proscribed faith, and by his want of training in a public school; but after all these deductions, we cannot but deplore the spectacle of one of the finest, clearest, and sharpest minds that England ever produced, so frequently reminding you of a bright sting set in the body, and steeped in the venom, of a wasp. And yet, withal, he possessed many virtues, which endeared him to a multitude of friends. He was a kind son. He was a faithful and devoted friend. He loved, if not man, yet many men with deep tenderness. A keen politician he was not; but, so far as he went along with his party, he was true to the common cause. In morals, he was greatly superior, in point of external decorum, to most of the wits of the time; but in falsehood, finesse, treachery, and envy, he stood at the bottom of the list, without that plea of poverty, or wretchedness, or despair, which so many of them might have urged. Uneasy, indeed, he always, and unhappy he often, was; but very much of his uneasiness and unhappiness sprung from his own fault. He attacked others, and could not bear to be attacked in return. He was a bully and a coward. He threw himself into a thorn-hedge, and was amazed that he came out covered with scratches and blood. While he shone in satirising many kinds of vice, he laid himself open to retort by his own want of delicacy. He, as well as Swift, was fond of alluding in his verse to polluted and forbidden things. There, and there alone, his taste deserted him; and there is something disgusting and unnatural in the combination of the elegant and the obscene—the coarse in sentiment and the polished in style. And whatever may be said for many of the amiable traits of the Man, there is very little to be said for the general tendency—so far as healthy morality and Christian principle are concerned—of the writings of the Poet.

Alexander Pope – A Concise Bibliography

The Major works
Pastorals (1709)
An Essay on Criticism (1711)
Messiah (1712)
The Rape of the Lock (1712 and enlarged in 1714)
Windsor Forest (1713)
Translation of the Iliad (1715-1720)
Eloisa to Abelard (1717)
Three Hours After Marriage, with others (1717)
Elegy to the Memory of an Unfortunate Lady (1717)
The Works of Shakespear, in Six Volumes (1723-1725)
Translation of the Odyssey (1725-1726)
Peri Bathous, Or the Art of Sinking in Poetry (1727)
The Dunciad (1728)
Essay on Man (1733-1734)
The Prologue to the Satires (1735)

www.ingramcontent.com/pod-product-compliance
Lightning Source LLC
Chambersburg PA
CBHW060147050426
42448CB00010B/2347